Luke's Jesus

Luke's Jesus

Between Incarnation and Crucifixion

JOSEPH BLENKINSOPP

FORTRESS PRESS
Minneapolis

LUKE'S JESUS
Between Incarnation and Crucifixion

Unless otherwise noted, the author considers all Scripture translations to be his own.

Cover image: St. Luke by Franz Hals (1582-1666), courtesy of Wikimedia Commons
Cover design: Savanah Landerholm

Print ISBN: 978-1-5064-7183-9
eBook ISBN: 978-1-5064-7184-6

CONTENTS

PREFACE

Does the scholarly world really need another commentary on the Gospel of Luke? Perhaps it does, but what follows is not a commentary on the third Gospel as that would generally be understood. And while I draw on the extensive scholarly literature on Luke and related topics, this book is not intended primarily for scholars. Rather, I am writing this book for the benefit of those whose interests in the Gospel of Luke are primarily theological and personal. My experiences as a scholar and teacher in the field of Old Testament studies have convinced me that biblical scholarship, at its best, can help illuminate the deeper meaning of Scripture by clearing away misunderstandings and bridging the gap between antiquity and our own times. In this book, I hope to allow Luke to speak with his own voice in order to offer his own distinctive witness to the life of Jesus of Nazareth.

I was motivated to write on this subject by a personal reading and frequent rereading of Luke's Gospel many years ago, which I found, and still find, to be the most interesting of the Gospels. The third evangelist tells the story of Jesus in terms that are clear, dramatically compelling, and humanly moving. His Jesus is a man of great power with a deep sense of mission, and at the same time, he has profound compassion for those on the outskirts of society. And Luke's Gospel has the best stories—that is, parables—including a number that are unique to him.

While writing, it occurred to me that I was working in the gap between "born of the virgin Mary" and "suffered under Pontius Pilate" in the Athanasian Creed, these texts representing the biographical extremes that attract so many lives of Jesus. In any case, it is usually important for those who write biography to report how the lives of their subjects began and ended, but with Luke we are traveling on more difficult terrain. For the birth of Jesus, there are two quite different scenarios in Matthew and Luke (Matt 2:1–13; Luke 2:1–20), while the conclusion to the life of Jesus as a member of the human race, as a *ben adam* (Hebrew: a "son of man"—i.e., a human being), ends neither with his death nor with his resurrection from the tomb but with his being taken up from the earth to the heavens to return and be with God his Father, an event recorded in the Acts of the Apostles, Luke's second work (Acts 1:9–11), a composition inspired by the "taking up" or "translation" of the great Northern prophet Elijah (read 2 Kgs 2:6–12).

My reading of the gospel is historical in its approach, for which I make no apologies. A historical reading of the Gospels follows necessarily from the Christian doctrine of the Incarnation, which implies that God has entered the history of humanity through Jesus. At the same time, this reading is also intended to be theological. Luke, together with the other evangelists, wants to show us that in the person of Jesus of Nazareth, God has drawn near to us in an inexpressible and unique way. He also has much to say about the nature and attributes of God the Father, especially in those delightful parables. God is portrayed throughout the Old and New Testaments as a warrior or a stern judge, but Luke, through his parables, presents God as a loving, anxious father who forgives his erring son before the boy can ask to be forgiven and lavishes love on him.

Throughout this reading, special attention will be given to the theme of wealth and poverty in the teaching of Jesus as presented by Luke. This book is not intended to be a study of Jesus's teachings on wealth and poverty as such, but no account of his teaching can fail to take note of the centrality of this theme. For Jesus, "the poor" included not only those who suffer economic deprivation but all those who are deprived—by poverty, illness, or social deprivation—of the chance of living a productive life in society. Jesus's public activities centered around bringing these people into full participation in the life of society, and he does so by preaching to the poor, healing those suffering from illness and disability, and reaching out to and reconciling sinners. At the same time, he made it clear that the rich—all those who think that their place in society is secure—risk the fate of the rich man who ignored Lazarus at his gate and, as a result, found himself exiled to Hades. This theme should induce reflection on some of our current social ills and dilemmas—in the first instance, the huge gap between the very wealthy and the poor, a situation normalized in many societies today.

If this approach to Luke's fascinating Gospel falls into the hands of readers who find in it new profit and new energy for living the Christian life, perhaps even pleasure in reading or rereading a Gospel, then this little book will have served its purpose.

PRINCIPAL ABBREVIATIONS

AB	Anchor Bible
ABD	Anchor Bible Dictionary
Ant	The Historian Josephus: Jewish Antiquities
ExpT	The Expository Times
JBL	Journal of Biblical Literature
JW	The Historian Josephus: The Jewish War
LXX	The Septuagint (Greek language version)
NRSV	New Revised Standard Version
NTS	New Testament Studies
REV	Revised English Version

I

THE AUTHOR

Luke

The Gospel of Luke is preeminent among the Gospels both canonical (Matthew, Mark, and John) and noncanonical. For our purposes, the most important among the latter is *The Gospel of Thomas*, a collection of sayings of a mystagogical or gnostic nature attributed to Jesus and discovered in Upper Egypt in 1945. In the first place, Luke's Gospel is a self-consciously structured literary and biographical work, recognizable as a life of Jesus. It is preeminent on the teachings of Jesus, conspicuously on the theme of wealth and poverty, the rich and the poor, the subject to which we will give special attention in our reading of this Gospel. It also has the best parables, including six major narrative parables to be found only in Luke, ending with the incomparable story of the rich man and Lazarus. For these and other reasons, we would like to be better acquainted with the author, but unfortunately, as with so many of the texts dealing with the beginnings of the Christian movement, obtaining solid information is not easy. Unlike some of the Pauline Epistles, the Gospels are not self-referential, though the author of the third Gospel at least speaks in the first person in the prologue to both the Gospel (Luke 1:1–4) and Acts of the Apostles (Acts 1:1–3), his second volume, but does so without giving his name. This two-volume work—the Gospel according to Luke and the Acts of the Apostles—would together make up the longest unit in the New Testament.

From the author's introduction to the Gospel, we gather that he was an educated man familiar with the conventions of Greek historiography and that his work was addressed to contemporary fellow Christians, especially proselytes like the Theophilus mentioned in both prologues. He mentions his sources—perhaps with a touch of depreciation for predecessors common in contemporary Greek historiography and biography. Among these many sources known to us, the best known are the Gospel of Mark and the source behind the matter common to both Matthew and Luke, the so-called Q (from the German *Quelle*, meaning "source"). Scholars usually list whatever in Luke cannot be traced to these two sources under the siglum L, meaning source material proper to Luke, though we know practically nothing about its place of origin and time of composition. Since these sources do not amount to the "many" of the prologue, we assume that the author had access to other sources of information about which we can only speculate. We know at least from his second volume that Luke had good information about the Judaic-Christian community in Jerusalem under the leadership of Peter, who acted as its spokesman, and James, brother of Jesus (Acts 12:17; 15:13; 21:18; Gal 1:19; 2:9, 11–12).

Behind these "many have undertaken to compile a narrative of the things which have been accomplished among us" (Luke 1:1) are the contemporaries of Jesus, the eyewitnesses and servants of the gospel, guardians and transmitters of the primordial tradition about Jesus. Building on this base, the author claims to have investigated everything from the beginning, which for him meant from the birth of John the Baptist followed soon afterward by the birth of Jesus, and to have proceeded from that point in an orderly manner. The prologue to Acts (1:1–3), Luke's second volume, is somewhat different. In referring to the author's first volume, it traces the narrative from the beginning of Jesus's public activity, ending not with his death and resurrection but with his "translation," or his final departure from his followers narrated in Acts 1:6–11 corresponding to the final paragraph in Luke's Gospel (24:50–52).[1] To sum up, though at a second or third remove from the lifetime of Jesus, the author of the third Gospel is, nevertheless, well informed and confident in his ability to undertake his self-appointed task.

As far as we know, questions about authorship began to be seriously addressed only in the second century CE, when curiosity about Christian origins was beginning to spread. Irenaeus, bishop of Lyons (ca. 130–200 CE) identified the author as Loukas (the Greek version of Luke), companion of Paul, mentioned in the Letter to Philemon verse 24 together with other disciples, including a colleague called Mark. Luke is also named in Colossians 4:14, where he is described as Paul's physician and dear friend. From about the same time as Irenaeus comes the earliest list of New Testament writings, known as the Muratorian Canon, so called because it was discovered in the Ambrosiana Library in Milan by a certain Father Muratori, an Italian priest. Published in 1740, it identifies Luke as the author. This was confirmed by the same name appearing at the end of the earliest extant manuscript of the Gospel, the papyrus codex cataloged as Papyrus Bodmer XVI. This could be the Luke who was the only one left with Paul during his captivity, probably in Rome (2 Tim 4:11). This appears to be the majority opinion, but some commentators have chosen instead to argue in favor of Loukios, identified as one of the leaders of the church in Antioch (now Antakya in Turkey), where, as some commentators maintain, Luke was born and educated. Finally, we have the "We" sections in the Acts of the Apostles, which suggest that the author of this work accompanied Paul on a hazardous sea journey from Troas, arriving eventually in Rome (Acts 16:10–17; 20:5–8, 13–15; 21:1–18; 27:1–28:16).

Without pursuing this further, we can say that the evidence for Luke as a companion of Paul is strong, though it is doubtful whether in speaking about "my gospel" in Romans 2:16, Paul was referring to the Gospel according to Luke, as some have suggested. In any case, these bits of information tell us little about the author apart from his name. We note that in writing to the Christian church at Colossae in Asia Minor, Paul added greetings from "Luke the beloved physician" (Col 4:14), which many have concluded is a reference to the author of the third Gospel. This may be so, but this conclusion—about the author as a physician—has not been confirmed by a close study of Luke's two-volume work.[2] A close relationship with Paul during his missionary journeys certainly arouses interest, but the author of the third Gospel does not seem to be closely familiar with any of the Pauline Epistles, and what is said about the law of Moses in the Gospel does not sound very Pauline. To go beyond this minimum, there is no alternative to a careful and close reading of the Gospel according to Luke and the Acts of the Apostles, and this is what we propose to do with what the first volume of Luke's two-volume work has to say, especially on issues of wealth and poverty, the rich and the poor, referring to the second volume as the occasion warrants.

Following Luke's brief summary of his work in the prologue, we will start "from the beginning" with an account of the birth and career of John, commonly called the Baptist;[3] the birth of Jesus presented in parallel with that of John, his cousin; and their close relationship with each other, which ended with the execution of John by Herod Antipas, son of Herod "the Great." There follows the preparatory time spent by each in the Judean wilderness; the Galilean ministry of Jesus, himself a Galilean; his encounters with different people friendly or hostile; and his healings, exorcisms, and miracles. This will serve as an introduction to his "Sermon on the Plain" (Luke 6:12–49) and other examples of his teaching addressed to those he encounters, also to his disciples and, indirectly, to fellow Christians of Luke's own generation. Finally, to those of us of a much later time who are willing to read, listen to the evangelist's voice, and learn.

Telling stories in the form of parables was, and perhaps also remains, one of the most powerful means of teaching by example how to live a good and productive life in the presence of God. The second section of the book will consist of a close reading of the six major parables unique to Luke, ending with the most memorable, the parable of the rich man and Lazarus (Luke 16:19–31).

2

THE SUBJECT

Jesus

First Impressions

The Gospel story is the story of Jesus told from different perspectives and at a certain distance from the events by authors for whom it had the greatest importance. Luke's version begins with a related story, that of John, known as the Baptist or Baptizer, who was a member of the same extended family as Jesus—probably a cousin, since John's mother, Elizabeth, was closely related to Mary, the mother of Jesus (in view of the difference in age, probably as aunt to niece).[1] Jesus enters the public sphere proclaiming the same message as John, the same message verbatim according to Matthew's Gospel, about the need to reconsider and change the direction of one's life—in other words, to repent.

Jesus acts with the assurance of a sleepwalker. He does the most amazing things in a matter-of-fact way, sometimes with anger not entirely suppressed, sometimes with pity or even a touch of dry humor. He tells cripples to get up and walk, and by God, they walk, maybe for the first time in their lives. He gently touches the eyes of the blind and they begin to see, either gradually or instantaneously. He has a passion for, and rage on behalf of, the poor and destitute and scorn or pity for those who spend their lives accumulating wealth. He can even walk on water. He said it: all you need is to believe, to really believe, and you can move mountains, you can change reality, create a new reality, beginning with yourself. Peter tried walking on water: he nearly made it, but when he began to have second thoughts, he started to go under. The story of our lives!

Jesus was not afraid to challenge authority. He was not cowed. Religious rules—like the Sabbath law, dietary matters, who you may or may not be at table with—are good and necessary insofar as they serve human needs, but only so far. It was this amazing freedom that led some in his circle of followers to believe that he was no ordinary religious leader, meaning that he must have a special relationship with God. Starting from this belief, it was not difficult for some of his followers to conclude that he had a unique relationship with God and, eventually, a shared identity. What they took this to mean was that who or what we call God could penetrate Jesus so fully, he was so transparent to God, that through him God could do what we all want our God to do: to heal our wounds and the wounds of others, to heal our pain and the pain of others, to reconcile ourselves to ourselves and others, and to forgive our sins. This, I believe, is the starting point of Christian theology and specifically of the doctrine of the Trinity articulated in the great church councils in a language no longer readily intelligible today. It is what another enthusiastic disciple of Jesus would mean when he said that God was reconciling the world to himself through Jesus (2 Cor 5:19). Perhaps it is still possible for us not only to believe this but even to reproduce some of the enthusiasm of Paul and other early witnesses to Jesus.

As for the miracles, they cannot be adequately described simply as Jesus doing something to a person, something inexplicable to those who witnessed it and perhaps even to us, who know so much more. A miracle of healing, for example, cannot be just a shortcut to a medical procedure. Perhaps all miracles are in some way transactional. Perhaps it wasn't just a case of acting directly on the afflicted subject. Perhaps Jesus had the capacity to awaken something in subjects so that those subjects could respond and contribute to their own healing and so act cocreatively. We note that in most if not all miracles, there is a demand for faith or at least a presumption of faith. Often, in fact, the faith or belief of the subject in Jesus is explicit. In the case of the Gerasene demoniac, the blind beggar, the leper, or whoever, Jesus had the capacity to coax something out of the subject, which, in turn, enabled the subject to cooperate with Jesus and, in so doing, change their life, often in unforeseeable ways.

The Early Years of John and Jesus

Luke's Jesus story begins with the birth and early years of John and then Jesus, often referred to as "Jesus of Nazareth," told along parallel lines.[2] For Luke, the Jesus story as a whole is closely interwoven with the appearance, public activity, and fate of John. Jesus was baptized by John (Luke 3:21–22) and, like John, he prepared for his life's work by spending some time in the wilderness (1:80; 4:1–13). According to the fourth Gospel, Jesus recruited his first disciples from John's followers—first Andrew and then his brother Simon, renamed Cephas, meaning "the Rock" (John 1:35–42). It is not beyond belief that Jesus himself was, for a time, a disciple of his cousin. There may be a suggestion of deliberate ambiguity in the way John identifies Jesus as "the one who comes after me" (Mark 1:7; Matt 3:11), which, in addition to temporal sequence, could be understood as "the one who follows me as a disciple follows his master." The ambiguity lies in the phrase "after me" (Greek: *opiso mou*); compare the statement of Jesus later in the Gospel: "Anyone wishing to come after me [*opiso mou*] must renounce self, take up his cross, and follow me" (Luke 9:23, my translation).[3]

At any rate, Mark's Gospel records that Jesus initiated his itinerant mission in Galilee only after John was imprisoned and therefore removed from the scene (Mark 1:14–15). According to the same source, Jesus began to predict his own violent death only after John had been executed by Herod Antipas, son of Herod the

Great, and the news of the execution had been brought to Jesus (6:17–32; 8:31–38). The long and detailed account of the execution of John in the Gospel according to Mark, a Gospel notably sparing of details, indicates that this event was a turning point in the public life of Jesus (6:17–29). It was only then that Jesus took pity on "sheep without a shepherd," meaning "the sheep deprived of a shepherd" (6:34), with reference to John. It seems that Jesus took over from John the role of public prophet, though the followers of John and Jesus eventually went their separate ways. The "Johannines" were ascetical, in contrast to the disciples of Jesus (Luke 7:33–34). In keeping with John's original message (Luke 3:7–9), they preached a strongly eschatological and judgment-oriented message of salvation—"the wrath to come . . . the axe . . . laid to the root of the trees" and similar language (3:7–9)—while for Jesus, the first stage toward salvation was to enable those shunned by society (especially on account of leprosy[4]) to rejoin society and, in general, for those with various disabilities, including and especially disabling poverty, to live a good and productive life here and now. As Jesus pointed out to the disciples sent by John, who apparently was no longer sure of the identity and role of Jesus, "The blind receive their sight, the lame walk, lepers are cleansed, and the deaf hear, the dead are raised up, the poor have good news preached to them" (Luke 7:22). We shall see that many of the miracles of Jesus have their rationale in the achievement of this salvific goal.

The importance for Luke of this earliest stage in the life and activity of John is emphasized by the way he places it in the larger historical and political framework of the Roman Empire: the birth of John during the reign of Herod, king of Judaea (37–4 BCE); the birth of Jesus during the reign of the emperor Augustus (27 BCE to 14 CE); and more fully, the appearance of John in the wilderness of Judaea in the fifteenth year of the reign of Tiberius (14–37 CE). At that time, Pilate was procurator of the Roman province of Judaea (26–36 CE), and Annas and Caiphas were the senior temple priests.

As for the birth date of Jesus, on the assumption that the Gospels are correct in placing this event during the lifetime of Herod (e.g., Luke 1:5), Jesus was born no later than the death of Herod in 4 BCE and very probably a few years earlier. Our distinction between BC and AD (or BCE and CE) we owe to the calculations of a Russian monk called Dionysius Exiguus (Denis the Little), who got it wrong by a few years.

The Law of Moses in Luke 1–2

Obedience to a written law was an important aspect of moral conduct at the time of Jesus, as it still is today for many Jews, Christians, and Muslims. It will therefore be necessary to bear this in mind in our investigation of what Luke has to say in his Gospel about moral issues, especially those connected with the theme of wealth and poverty. It is interesting that the law of Moses is more clearly in evidence in Luke's account of the birth and early years of John and Jesus in the first two chapters than it is in the rest of the Gospel. The first thing we learn about John's parents, the priest Zachariah and his wife Elizabeth, is that they conducted their lives according to all the commandments and precepts of the Lord God (Luke 1:6). Jesus is circumcised in keeping with immemorial customs confirmed by the law (2:21; Lev 12:3). Mary, his mother, undergoes the rite of postpartum purification and offers the gift prescribed by the law for those of modest means (2:22–24; Lev 12:1–9). As firstborn, Jesus is presented in the temple according to the law (Luke 2:27; Num 18:15–16), and in concluding this first phase of the story of Jesus, Luke tells us that "the parents brought in the child Jesus, to do for him according to the custom of the law" (Luke 2:27–29).

We may assume further that the family of Jesus was also exemplary in keeping the great festivals, since they made the long journey from Nazareth to Jerusalem every year to celebrate Passover in the temple (Luke 2:41). The temple with its liturgies formed the other pillar of Judaic religious life together with the law of Moses. Luke's Gospel begins with John's parents in the temple, the presentation of Jesus there, and his eventual discovery in the temple, "his Father's house," by his anxious parents.[5] The Gospel ends with the disciples of Jesus returning to Jerusalem after the risen Jesus has parted from them. The last verse of the Gospel reads, "They returned to Jerusalem with great joy, and were continually in the temple blessing God" (24:53). Read from this perspective, Luke's Gospel is a record of the process by which the good news proclaimed by Jesus was extended to all peoples beyond the legal and religious boundaries of the Judaism of that time. Viewed from a different perspective, that of social organization, it could be read as a record of the progress of the disciples of Jesus from being a movement within Israel, comparable in some respects to the Pharisees, to being a distinct and distinctive religious movement open in principle to anyone outside of the legal bounds of Israel. The early stages of that transformation are recorded in Luke's second volume.

Jesus Messiah

The most ambiguous of the titles assigned to Jesus in the third Gospel, the Acts of the Apostles, and elsewhere in the New Testament is Messiah, or *māshîah* in Hebrew, with reference to a person (or, much less commonly, a place of worship) anointed with sacred oil for a particular purpose or mission. Priests were anointed in this manner (see, e.g., Lev 4 and 6), and the book of Daniel refers to the time allotted for the resacralization by anointment of the Jerusalem temple after it had been defiled by the ruler Antiochius II (Dan 9:24). The most prominent among those anointed, however, was the reigning monarch, beginning in Israel with Saul (1 Sam 24:4–7; 26:9, 23) and then, preeminently, David (2 Sam 22:51; 23:1; Pss 2; 18; 27, etc.). This continues into New Testament usage, but the situation now is that the title for the anointed one in Greek is χριστος (*christos*), from the verb χριϖ (anoint), which creates confusion with what has become a common way of referring to Jesus with a composite name, Jesus Christ. This makes it necessary to attend carefully to the context wherever this form appears.

Coming back to Luke's Gospel, in the Lukan account of the birth of Jesus and his early years, which ended with baptism by John the Baptist (Luke 1:1–3:38), there is a strong emphasis on the future kingship of Jesus as a descendant of David and therefore on Jesus as a royal messiah, a theme that is far less prominent in the encounters of his adult life, beginning with his mission in Galilee, and is by no means accepted unequivocally by Jesus. In the narrative of his birth and early years, on the contrary, it is present throughout. He is announced by the angel Gabriel to Mary as the Son of the Most High who will occupy the throne of David, his ancestor, and reign over Israel forever (1:26–33). Elizabeth, wife of the priest Zechariah, welcomes the visit of her lord and master—in fact, her king—though he is still in Mary's womb (1:43–45). A similar note can be heard in the antiphons attributed to other characters in the drama of the birth of Jesus, including Mary's antiphon, known from its opening word as the Magnificat (1:46–55). Most significant in this respect is the urgency of Joseph, himself of Davidic descent, to take his wife, already very pregnant, on a three-day journey from Nazareth in Galilee to Bethlehem in Judah so that Jesus the Messiah will first see the light of day in "the little town of Bethlehem," closely associated with David, thereby fulfilling an event foretold long before by the prophet Micah:

From you, Bethlehem in Ephrathah,
small as you are among Judah's clans,
from you will come a king for me over Israel,
one whose origins are far back in the past, in ancient times.
(Mic 5:2 REB)

In this first section of the Gospel of Luke, Jesus is recognized and acclaimed by other titles—"Son of God" (1:35; 4:3), "Beloved Son" (3:22), and "Lord Most High" (1:12, 43, 68; 2:23)—all consistent with the titulature of royalty in Israel.

In Luke's presentation of the public activity of Jesus, which can be dated from his baptism by John, John was already known far and wide for his preaching about the final judgment at the end time, for which they were to prepare by immersion in the purifying water of baptism, leading to sincere repentance. John's fame was such that many regarded him as the Messiah. John, however, insisted that his task was limited to preparing the way for the one who would come as savior and judge at the end of the age, a role to be filled by Jesus. Perhaps John had a premonition that his mission would be brought to an end by the current ruler, Herod Antipas, maybe at the insistence of his masters in Rome, or perhaps he was persuaded by the extraordinary circumstances accompanying the baptism of Jesus: the descent of the dove, symbol of the spirit of God, and the voice that proclaimed Jesus as God's beloved Son (Luke 3:21–22).

The fame of Jesus as preacher and worker of miracles would inevitably have come to the attention of Herod Antipas, second son of Herod the Great. Both father and son were no doubt sensitive to the possibility of someone like John or Jesus causing a public disturbance, which might come to the attention of their Roman masters. So they were interested to find out the identity of this Jesus, known as a miracle worker and advocate for the poor. Some informants thought he must be John the Baptist come back from the dead or maybe a reincarnation of one of the ancient prophets, like Elijah or Elisha. None of this satisfied Antipas: "John I beheaded; but who is this about whom I hear such things?" (Luke 9:7–9).

At about the same time, Jesus was asking his disciples to tell him what people were saying about him, who they thought he was. The answer was the same as the one that failed to convince Herod Antipas—namely, that he was John, Elijah, or some other prophet come back to life in the body of Jesus. Then Jesus asked his disciples who they thought he was. As expected, the impetuous Peter answered for all: God's Messiah (Luke 9:20). The answer was correct, but Peter must have been surprised to hear Jesus forbidding his disciples from making public use of this title. From that point on, they were to keep in view his coming rejection by the local authorities, his suffering, and his death. He was to be known not as

Messiah or Son of God but as Son of Man (*ben adam*), a title that connotes his humanity. In Hebrew, this second title signifies at the most basic level "a human being," but for Jesus at that moment, it signified a human being destined to suffer rejection and death at the hands of other human beings.

3

FAMILY, SOCIAL STATUS, AND WEALTH

The Families of Jesus

We have seen that John and Jesus belonged to the same extended family, though scattered widely in Judaea and Galilee. The nuclear family with which Jesus passed his early years was quite large. The Gospels refer to four brothers of Jesus—James, Joseph (or Joses, a kind of nickname), Simon, and Judah—and several unnamed sisters. The people in the Nazareth synagogue knew that he was the son of a carpenter and therefore not of high social status, and they knew four brothers by name and all his sisters. Among those present at the crucifixion of Jesus, the Gospel of John numbers the following: Mary, his mother; Mary's sister, the aunt of Jesus, who is unnamed; Mary, wife of Klopas;[1] and Mary from Magdala, a village on the Sea of Galilee. Since issues of poverty and wealth are often predetermined by the family into which one is born, we start with family. Neither family, of John or of Jesus, seems to have been poor in any obvious sense. Zechariah, John's father, was a priest employed by the Jerusalem temple, a wealthy, well-endowed institution, while Joseph, the father of Jesus (and perhaps also Jesus himself for a time) was a woodworker or carpenter (Matt 13:55; Mark 6:3). They therefore belonged to the artisan class, hence people of modest but adequate means. *Poverty* is a relative term, one indication of which is the rich vocabulary for "the poor" in the Hebrew Bible.[2] It can refer to a family or individual lacking the essentials of life or reduced to begging, like Lazarus in the parable, but also to a family like Joseph, Mary, Jesus, and his brothers and sisters, who could afford to make the three-day journey from Galilee to Jerusalem year after year for the celebration of Passover (Luke 2:41) while apparently owning no significant assets, land being the crucial factor. Jesus was born in a manger according to Luke (2:7, 12), but only because there was no room for them in the local inn, while in Matthew's Gospel, the magi, learned members of the elite wherever they came from, visited the newborn Jesus in a house (Matt 2:11). On the other hand, in fulfilling the ritual of postpartum purification, Mary offered a pair of turtledoves or pigeons instead of a lamb or goat, the concession provided in the law for those of more modest means (Luke 2:22–24, based on Lev 5:7; 12:6–8). The impression, therefore, is that the family of Jesus did not possess the wealth that came with owning land or similar assets, but neither were they poor and needy.

Wealth, as exhibited by expensive clothing and a well-filled table—like the rich man in the parable dressed in purple and fine linen who feasted sumptuously (Luke 16:19)—is generally considered an essential prerequisite for social status, as we well know. Unfortunately, however, the story of Jesus's life told by Luke does not provide much information on the social status of Jesus. At the beginning of his public activity, Jesus was permitted to read and preach on the *haftarah* (the reading from the Prophets) in the Nazareth synagogue, though lacking the usual qualifications, and the hearers were astonished, since they knew him to be the son of a local carpenter called Joseph (Luke 4:16–30). In the Capernaum synagogue, likewise, the hearers were surprised, since Jesus was not known as a trained preacher (4:31–37).

After he left his family behind, Jesus came to be recognized as a prophet, miracle worker, and "holy man," like his predecessor, Honi the Circle-Drawer, about a century earlier, and his near-contemporary,

Hanina ben Dosa, also a Galilean.[3] Honi (Onias) was known for an original form of prayer. During a drought, he drew a circle on the ground, stood in it, and told God he would stay in it and, if necessary, die in it, unless God sent rain, which God did. Hanina ben Dosa, active in the decade preceding the war with Rome, which ended with the destruction of the temple, was a Galilean worker of miracles comparable to those of Jesus and the author of a collection of sayings. These are important components of a Gospel as we know Gospels, but with Hanina, they never came together, so there is no Gospel of Hanina ben Dosa.

More often than not, Jesus was addressed as a teacher (*didaskalos*), and this recognition put him on a par with Pharisees, scribes, and other educated people. Though sometimes hostile, Pharisees acknowledged Jesus's gifts, and some even invited him as a guest for a meal (Luke 7:36–49; 11:37–41). He was, however, on better terms with tax collectors, two of whom—Levi (5:27–32) and Zacchaeus (19:1–10)—are named in Luke. The tax collectors—then, as now, not held in the highest regard by the common people, especially since many of them worked for the Roman overlord—accepted John's baptism of repentance, unlike the Pharisees, who refused it (3:12–13; 7:29–30).

Jesus and "Family Values"

This brings us to the much-discussed issue of "family values." None of the Gospel writers manifests much enthusiasm for Jesus's immediate family, with the exception of his mother. After preaching in the Nazareth synagogue, the reputation of Jesus was not improved when the locals recalled that he was the son of a carpenter, brother of James, Joseph (or Joses), Judas, and Simon, as well as several unnamed sisters (Matt 13:55–56; Mark 6:3; cf. Luke 4:22). According to John's Gospel, his brothers even urged him to leave his hometown of Nazareth for Jerusalem adding, with a touch of sarcasm, "so that your followers may see the great things you are doing" (John 7:1–4, my paraphrase). Even they, the writer adds, had no faith in him (John 7:5). On another occasion, after the calling of the Twelve, Jesus entered a house, and once more a crowd gathered around him so that Jesus and his disciples couldn't even get a bite to eat. When his family members heard of his activities, they set out to detain him, fearing that he was out of his mind (Mark 3:20–21), which, in that culture, was not far removed from the charge of possession by a malevolent spirit (Luke 11:15). On another occasion, his mother and brothers were trying to get to him through the crowd. On being told by some close to him that "your mother and your brothers are standing outside, desiring to see you," Jesus replied, "My mother and my brothers are those who hear the word of God and do it" (Luke 8:19–21) or, as more fully reported in Matthew 12:46–50, "Stretching out his hand toward his disciples, he said, 'Here are my mother and my brothers! For whoever does the will of my Father in heaven is my brother, and sister, and mother.'"

Like so much in Luke's Gospel, such categorical statements illustrate Luke's habit of presenting views and opinions in the form of opposites, antitheses, or reversals. For example, in the previously mentioned parable of the rich man and Lazarus, a conspicuously wealthy man is judged by Jesus not so much by his wealth as in relation to a poor and sick beggar. In Luke's Gospel, moral issues are predominantly relational. In the same way, family members are viewed over against those called out of their families into discipleship, the new family of disciples. The point is made in Luke's presentation of three case histories of aspirants to discipleship (Luke 9:57–62). The first is reminded that the Son of Man has nowhere to lay his head—in other words, he has no home and no family life—so you must live in the same way. The second makes what appears to be a reasonable request to bury his father before following Jesus—which probably implied caring for him in the final stage of his life—and is told to "let the dead bury their dead." The request of the third to say goodbye to his family receives an equally peremptory response using an agrarian metaphor: no one who puts his hand to the plow and then looks back—to family, home, and a peaceful and comfortable domestic existence—is fit for the kingdom of God.

Something similar should be assumed for the most categorical statement about family in the Gospels: "If any one comes to me and does not hate his own father and mother and wife and children and brothers and sisters . . . he cannot be my disciple" (Luke 14:26). The parallel version in Matthew 10:37 is often interpreted as a mitigation of the Lukan text, which is probably correct. Apropos of this disturbing saying, it should be noted that the Hebrew verb for hating (*śānaʾ*) occurs also in the legal or quasi-legal sense of dissociation without any necessary implication of negative emotion. It is used, for example, to distinguish between the legally binding inheritance rights of the infertile woman (*śĕnûʾāh*, literally "the hated one") and those of the one who bears children (*ʾăhûbāh*, "the loved one"), again without any necessary emotional content (Gen 29:31–33; Deut 21:15–17). Another example comes from the records of the Judaic colony on the island of Elephantine at the first cataract of the Nile in the fifth century BCE. In a deed of divorce (*dîn śānāh*), the statement "I hate my wife" was not a final angry retort by the former husband; it served simply as a legal formula that formalized and closed the proceedings.[4]

At any rate, it is impossible to imagine that Jesus hated his family, even though some of them didn't understand his mission and may have been opposed to it. Active participation in the mission of Jesus in any capacity called for the renunciation of family life with its many consolations, but it led to the formation of an alternative family, the gathering of men and women willing to renounce the comforts, consolations, and rewards of family life in order to follow Jesus. Those who did so embodied the alternative community that God is gathering to himself at all times, known in Isaiah and Psalms as "the servants of the Lord" and "the poor."

A New Family on the Road

Once Jesus left his own family behind, he and his disciples led a peripatetic existence in keeping with the norms laid down for the mission of the Twelve and the Seventy-Two (Luke 9:1–6; 10:1–12). Being constantly on the move is a precarious way to live, but Jesus and his disciples were fortunate to have the services of a dedicated band of women who attended to the material needs of the group. We have the names of a few of these remarkable women: Mary of Magdala; Susanna (Hebrew "Lily"); Mary, mother of James; Salome; and Joanna, wife of one of Herod Antipas's stewards and therefore probably well-to-do (Luke 8:1–3). These women proved to be more devoted to Jesus than his male disciples, since, unlike the latter, some of them stayed with him to the end. In Matthew's Gospel, the women present at the crucifixion of Jesus include Mary of Magdala; Mary, mother of James and Joseph; and the mother of the sons of Zebedee (Matt 27:55–56), but none of the Twelve. In John's Gospel, those present include Mary, mother of Jesus; her unnamed sister, the aunt of Jesus; Mary, wife of Klopas; and Mary of Magdala, the first to see Jesus arisen from the tomb and alive (John 20:1–18). The only male follower of Jesus present was the enigmatic beloved disciple. Mark 15:40–41 adds Salome among those who accompanied Jesus from Galilee. In Luke's Gospel, these women stood at a distance but then followed Joseph of Arimathaea as he buried Jesus, noted how the body was laid out, and prepared spices and perfumes to anoint the body after the Sabbath rest. On returning to the tomb on the first day of the week, they found it empty and had a vision of angels who reminded them of the prediction of Jesus about his death and resurrection on the third day. They reported this to the disciples gathered in a room in the city but were not believed. Named are Mary of Magdala, Joanna, and Mary, mother of James (Luke 23:49, 55; 24:10–11).

Some of these women may have become disciples in the more restricted sense of the term, since women were present in the upstairs room in Jerusalem together with Peter, the other disciples, and the mother of Jesus after Jesus had left them (Acts 1:12–14). The presence of these women together with the male disciples in Jesus's itinerant mission, especially after his fateful decision to go to Jerusalem (Luke 9:51–62), makes it easier to think of them as members of an alternative family, the family that in a special way responds to the call of God and strives to fulfill it in their daily lives (Luke 8:19–21; Isa 56:6; 65:8–9, 13–16; 66:14; Pss 22:26–27; 60:30–33; 147:6; 149:4).

In general, it is remarkable, given the culture of that time and place, how often in Luke's two-volume work women act and speak in their own right.

4

JOHN AND JESUS

Preparation in the Wilderness

Since the Israelite priesthood was hereditary, it was expected that John, offspring of the priest Zechariah and of a mother descended from Aaron, the first high priest, would follow in his father's footsteps as a priest in the temple; this was the issue behind the discussion of his name at his circumcision (Luke 1:59–63). However, soon after he was at the age of independence, he was to be found not in the temple but in the Judean wilderness, where he remained until he made his public appearance (1:80). However this came about, it calls for some disambiguation. One doesn't just wander about or "hang out" in the Judean Desert, one of the most inhospitable places in the world. Some years later, the Judaic historian Flavius Josephus, wishing to experience life in the different sects and conventicles—or so he tells us—spent time in his teens in the Judean Desert, living in the hermitage of a certain Bannus, who practiced the simple life: clothes made of the bark or leaves from trees, food growing naturally in that environment, and frequent ablutions in cold water (Josephus, *Life* 11–12). This is a regime that may have suggested John's diet of locusts and wild honey and his rough coat of camel's hair with a leather belt (Mark 1:6; Matt 3:4), the outfit in imitation of the great northern prophet Elijah (2 Kgs 1:8).

A more likely pied-à-terre for John in the wilderness, and a more appropriate preparation for his mission, would have been the Qumran settlement on the northwest shore of the Dead Sea, which by that time had been in existence for more than a century. John's way of life and his mission have much in common with those of the people of the Dead Sea Scrolls. These sectarians practiced frequent lustrations, or "baptisms" (immersions); lived in anticipation of a coming day of judgment and salvation; and in their community rule emphasized the necessity of repentance in preparation for the last day, the day of salvation and judgment (1QS 4:18–23).[1] Their practice of community of property is one of several features, including celibacy, a common meal, and ritual bathing, which have led many scholars to identify this community as a branch of the Essene sect (1QS I:11–12; V 1–2; VI 17–22). In his treatise *Every Good Man Is Free*, the philosopher Philo remarked of this sect that "in no other community do we find the custom of sharing roof, life, and board more firmly established" (§86). On the egalitarian lifestyle of the Essenes, Josephus says much the same: "Their community of goods is truly admirable; you will not find one among them distinguished by greater opulence than another" (*War* II 122; similar statements can be found in *Ant* XVIII 20). Pliny also tells us that the Essenes lived without money.[2] It seems that the members of the Qumran *yahad* (Hebrew for "a people united," "a community") set out to create a model and ideal for the people of Israel as a whole, "the community (*yahad*) of the tribes of Israel" of Deuteronomy 33:5 (my translation). The idea was to form an alternative society that would demonstrate the possibility of creating a genuinely egalitarian way of life in the society as a whole, in keeping with injunctions in the ancient law books (Lev 25:35–38; Deut 15:4). The coexistence of great wealth with great poverty, familiar to us today, could have no place in such a community.

If, then, John was in the Judean Desert until he received his call to prepare for his mission, and if he was received into the Qumran community, or a similar settlement—though we know of none other in that place and at that time—it seems that his intent was to take the community's ideal of a society in which there were no extremes of wealth and poverty out into the public sphere. His reply to the question put to him by individuals among those who responded to his message of repentance in preparation for the coming judgment—What then are we to do?—is found only in Luke and is remarkable for its down-to-earth simplicity: "He who has two coats, let him share with him who has none; and he who has food, let him do likewise" (Luke 3:11). This could, with some exegetical license, be read as a specific application of the Essenic and Qumranic insistence on the sharing of property. At the same time, it colors all of Luke's teaching on wealth and poverty. The Jesus of Luke will, in fact, take it a step further in his often counterintuitive teaching: "From him who takes away your coat do not withhold even your shirt" (6:29). A version of this ideal, mandated by John and followed by the Jesus of Luke's Gospel, was practiced by the disciples gathered in Jerusalem after Jesus had left them: "All who believed were together and had all things in common; and they sold their possessions and goods and distributed them to all, as any had need" (Acts 2:44–45). And further, "The company of those who believed were of one heart and soul, and no one said that any of the things which he possessed was his own, but they had everything in common. . . . There was not a needy person among them, for as many as were possessors of lands or houses sold them, and brought the proceeds of what was sold and laid it at the apostles' feet; and distribution was made to each as any had need" (Acts 4:32–35). There follow examples of both the practice and its violation involving, respectively, Joseph Barnabas, a Cypriot, and a couple, Ananias and Sapphira (4:36–5:11).

John's message, addressed to all listeners, is followed by two specific applications, perhaps chosen by Luke from a greater number handed down to him. Tax collectors are not to exact more than what is assessed; military personnel are to make do with their wages and not try to extort money by threats or false accusations (Luke 3:10–14). In short, do your job well and be thoughtful, just, and kind toward those with whom your work brings you into contact.

These applications are examples of John's mission to lead people to repentance, a change of life, in the spirit of Isaiah:

> *A voice cries:*
> *"In the wilderness prepare the way of the Lord,*
> *Make straight in the desert a highway for our God.*
> *Every valley shall be lifted up,*
> *and every mountain and hill be made low. . . .*
> *And the glory of the Lord shall be revealed,*
> *and all flesh shall see it together." (Isa 40:3–5)*[3]

Accepting baptism at John's hands therefore implied acceptance of the call to repentance and a willingness to make it effective in the conduct of the daily life of the initiate.

Following John's example, Jesus spent some time alone in the Judean wilderness preparing for his mission. Luke's genealogy of Jesus (3:23–38) interrupts the connection between his baptism by John, during which the Holy Spirit entered into him (3:21–22), and his decision, under the guidance of the same Spirit, to undertake his mission in Galilee, his own country, after retreating into the wilderness to prepare himself for it in the same way as his cousin did. This language of the spirit is the language of the great prophets of Israel, and the implication is that Jesus is modeling his ministry on theirs.

During his stay in the wilderness of Judaea, Jesus was tested, or tempted, by Satan to break his forty-day fast (Luke 4:1–4). Jesus replied by bringing up the testing of the ancestors by hunger in another wilderness, ending with a citation from Deuteronomy 8:3: "Man does not live by bread alone."[4] Fasting would seem to place Jesus in line with the asceticism practiced by John's followers and the Pharisees, though in the course of time, the difference between John's group and the disciples of Jesus with respect to fasting and other practices was apparently common knowledge (Luke 5:33; 7:33–34). In the second test, the Evil One, who claimed to be the supreme ruler of the world (a claim that is not disputed), appears to be attempting to recruit Jesus as his viceroy and representative on earth, with the promise of power, prestige, and wealth attached (Luke 4:5–8). This is refuted by an appeal to the first commandment of the Decalogue (Deut 5:9; 6:13).

The third test is somewhat obscure. Perhaps it is an invitation to display the miraculous power (Luke 4:9–11) attributed by many to the royal Messiah and to do so in the sight of all in the most conspicuous place in the holy city, the roof of the temple. After all, a rabbinic saying has it that "when the King Messiah reveals himself, he will come and stand on the roof of the temple" (*Pesiqta rabbati* §36). Since this does not in itself call for a miracle, perhaps the point of the test was not just standing on the roof but jumping off of it assisted by angels and surviving the fall as proof of miraculous messianic power.

In sum, Luke is at pains to emphasize the links between John and Jesus, the impetus that John provided for the mission of Jesus, and the continuities between the teachings of John and those of Jesus, especially with regard to wealth and poverty.

5

JESUS THE MIRACLE WORKER

Miracles in General

From New Testament times, and even earlier in recorded history, miraculous events were accepted without demur as divine interventions in human affairs either for good or for evil, though at times it was questioned whether a miracle had actually taken place. This rather obvious problem with miracles was raised by Thomas Hobbes in the thirteenth chapter of his *Leviathan*. He took the trouble to point out that events claimed to be miraculous may turn out to be something very different so that, as he put it, "all the miracle consisteth in is this, that the enchanter has deceived someone, which is no miracle but a very easie matter to doe." He added that for an event to be miraculous, it is not enough for it to be remarkable or unprecedented—for example, that a horse or cow speak—but it must also be purposeful and significative. In other words (he was writing about biblical miracles), it must aim to "beget or confirm beleefe" or "serve for the procuring of credit to God's messengers, ministers and prophets."[1]

Beginning with the Enlightenment, the biblical and especially New Testament miracles were subject to critical and often hostile philosophical scrutiny as being either in violation of the laws of nature (Spinoza, Locke, Hume), historically fictive and unreliable

(Reimarus), or at least unverifiable (Hegel). We cannot pursue this line of investigation, but in our reading of these texts, we will assume that, first, the miracle texts in the Gospels are worded by the authors to be intelligible to their hearers or readers but are not fictions created by either Luke or one or other of his sources; second, for the reader who is a person of faith, the power of God can intervene in human affairs and, in doing so, modify the course of nature; and third: in the last analysis, it is inevitable that each reader will interpret the Gospel miracles according to their own religious or philosophical convictions.[2]

Miracles of Jesus in Luke's Gospel

If, as Hobbes insisted, to be a miracle an event must be purposeful and significant, we should note that of the twenty such events in Luke's Gospel, eleven are miracles of healing, some remarkable only in being instantaneous; four are exorcisms; three are done to promote well-being or to save someone from danger; and two record the restoring to life of the dead: one the son of a widow and the other the daughter of a synagogue official.[3] We might contrast them with the miracles that the Tempter challenged Jesus to perform during his retreat in the wilderness: to turn stones into loaves of bread and to jump off the roof of the temple and land unharmed. These would have been like the speaking horse or cow of Hobbes: without obvious purpose or significance. The miracles of Jesus were quite different; we might think of them as the power of God flowing through Jesus to fulfill his mission, recalling once again the answer Jesus gave to the question of John's disciples about his identity: "Go and tell John what you have seen and heard: the blind receive their sight, the lame walk, lepers are cleansed, and the deaf hear, the dead are raised up" (Luke 7:22). To make this point more clearly, Luke has prefaced the visit of John's disciples with the raising to life of the dead son of a widow in Naim, a nearby town (7:11–17).

At this point, it will be helpful to take a closer look at one or two examples, beginning with the healing of the Roman centurion's servant (Luke 7:1–10). The miracle takes place in Capernaum and is therefore a continuation of Jesus's activity in the same town recorded earlier (4:31–44). It belongs to the category of miracle at a distance, or in absentia, which adds another degree of the wonderful and inexplicable to the act. The petitioner is a Roman centurion, but the petition is made by elders on behalf of the centurion and his servant, who is seriously ill and at the point of death.[4] They claim that he deserves this favor because he is sympathetic to local interests and had even financed the building of the local synagogue. He was one of the good Romans. Jesus accompanied the centurion and his friends to his lodgings, but in deference to Jesus, the centurion declared his house to be unworthy of such a distinguished guest. All Jesus had to do was say the word and the cure would come about, a point the centurion then illustrated by an interesting if not entirely relevant military analogy. Astonished by his unconditional belief in the certainty of the outcome, Jesus exclaimed to those around him, "I tell you, not even in Israel have I found such faith" (7:9). When the messengers, not yet convinced, went back into the house, they found the servant in good health.

Another version of the same miracle can be found in Matthew 8:5–13. In this Matthean version, the miracle also takes place in Capernaum, the petitioner is an equally deferential centurion who believes in the ability of Jesus to work a miracle of healing in the absence of the sufferer, and he elicits from Jesus the same surprise about his faith, expressed in the same words, though with additions (Matt 8:11–12). The differences are equally apparent. The centurion makes his appeal directly not through intermediaries as in Luke, the sufferer appears to be a son rather than a servant, the illness is identified as paralysis, and the simultaneity of the word of Jesus and the healing is stated explicitly.

Another close parallel can be found in John 4:46–54. The location is now Cana, where Jesus changed water into wine, but the sick child is in Capernaum, and the petitioner is a royal official, of what rank and in whose service we are not told. The basic narrative structure is identical, though here, too, the petitioner pleads directly and even when initially rebuffed keeps on insisting on the need for Jesus's help. As in the other variants, and indeed in practically all the miracles, the essential element is faith: in the first place, faith in Jesus himself and his power to heal. Finally, in this Johannine version, the simultaneity of the healing word of Jesus and the healing at a distance is emphasized with the greatest precision. The healing of the sufferer at the point of death takes place at the same time as Jesus tells the official, "Your son will live"; it was exactly 1 p.m.

While this first miracle was to the benefit of a sick individual, the second features a young man, a widow's son, who had died and was about to be buried. As Jesus was approaching the entrance to Naim (or Nain), not far from Capernaum, accompanied by his disciples and a great crowd anxious for contact with Jesus, they encountered a funeral procession leaving the town on its way to the burial ground outside the town limits. The deceased was the only son of his mother, and she was accompanied by many friends and acquaintances from the town. The decision to narrate this particular miracle, among so many other miracles of Jesus known to Luke, was no doubt dictated by the reply of Jesus to John's delegation, which included, in addition to bringing health to the sick and good news to the poor, bringing the dead back to life (Luke 7:22).

When Jesus saw the bereaved mother, he told her not to cry. He came forward, and when he laid his hand on the bier, the bearers halted. Then it happened. He spoke to the deceased: "Young man, I say to you, arise" (7:14), and the young man sat up and began to speak. We can only imagine the consternation and thrill of fear of the bystanders. Then Jesus gave him to his mother. Then someone blurted out, "A great prophet has arisen among us! . . . God has visited his people!" (7:16). It is hardly surprising that the account of what Jesus had done spread rapidly throughout all Judaea and the surrounding country.

Readers familiar with the marvelous stories about Elijah and his disciple, Elisha, in the Old Testament will, on reflecting on these miracles of Jesus, recall an incident that may have been in the minds of some of those who actually witnessed the miracle and praised God for a great prophet who had appeared among them. The incident in question is recorded in 1 Kings 17:8–24. It tells how, in his travels, Elijah came to a town called Zarephath on the Phoenician coast about fifty miles north of Mount Carmel. There the weary prophet was fed and given a room and a bed for the night by a pious widow in the town. Then tragedy struck: her son, perhaps her only son, took ill and died. The woman wondered whether this great misfortune may have been caused in some way by the presence in her house of this extraordinary man of God. In her grief, she even went so far as to accuse Elijah of bringing this tragedy upon her as punishment for unnamed sins. It was well known that these "men of God" could be a source of danger or even death to those who approached them. There is, for example, the incident in which some rude boys mocked Elisha, Elijah's disciple. Rather than ignoring them, he cursed them and sicced two bears on them, which left forty-two of them dead (2 Kgs 2:23–25); we might call it a classic case of overreaction.[5] Elijah's response to the woman was quite different. He took the dead child to his room, where he prayed and, while praying, stretched himself three times over the child's body. The child revived, Elijah gave him to his mother, and this astonishing incident concludes with the mother's profession of faith in Elijah and Elijah's God: "Now I know that you are a man of God, and that the word of the Lord in your mouth is truth" (1 Kgs 17:24).

There can be little doubt that the account of the resuscitation of the widow's son by Jesus in Nain is modeled on this story of Elijah. Jesus's encounter with the widow and her son took place at the entrance to Nain, and the encounter of Elijah with the widow and her son came about at the entrance of Zarepheth (1 Kgs 17:10; Luke 7:12); Jesus gave the son who had passed from death to life back to his mother as Elijah did, and he did so using the same words (1 Kgs 17:25; Luke 7:15); finally, both incidents conclude with a profession of belief that what they had witnessed was a gracious intervention of the God of Israel in human affairs brought about by means of his chosen servants (1 Kgs 17:24; Luke 7:16).

There are similar accounts of miracles worked by Jesus in Luke's Gospel, and some also in the Acts of the Apostles worked by Peter and Paul, but we will consider only one more in Luke, which balances the raising to life of a son on behalf of a mother with the raising of a daughter requested by a father (Luke 8:40–42, 49–56).[6] This father's name was Jairus (Hebrew: *Yā'îr*), president of the local synagogue, and he was desperate for help because his twelve-year-old daughter was dying. He begged Jesus to come and save her, but the crowds following Jesus made progress to the house difficult, and progress was further delayed when a woman who had been suffering from hemorrhages for twelve years touched the edge of Jesus's cloak and was instantly cured (8:42b–48). Then someone came from the house with the news that the girl had died, so there was no further need to trouble Jesus, here addressed as "the Teacher." Ignoring the bad news from the house, Jesus exhorted the people to really believe that she would be well again. On arrival at the house, he continued in the same strain. He asked the many mourners to hush their weeping and wailing, since, he said, "she is not dead; she is just asleep," a statement greeted with incredulous laughter by the mourners. On arrival in the room where the president's daughter was lying, into which he permitted entry only to the parents of the child and Peter, John, and James, the inner circle of the Twelve, Jesus held her hand and called out to her, "Wake up, child!"—almost like a simple wake-up call.[7] In response to his call, we are told, her spirit returned, she at once stood up, and Jesus calmly advised the parents that because she would be hungry, they should give her something to eat (John 8:51–55).

In summary, Luke records twenty miracles of Jesus, eleven of which are miracles of healing on behalf of people suffering from a serious disease (fever, epilepsy, dropsy, leprosy) or disability (paralysis, lameness); four are exorcisms; three are acts of benevolence (stilling a storm on Lake Kinneret, enabling a huge catch of fish, feeding more than five thousand people with five loaves of bread and two fishes); and two, the most remarkable, involve restoring the dead to life (the widow's son and Jairus's daughter). Most belong to the Galilean ministry; only five occur after the turning point in the narrative with the decision to leave Galilee and go to Jerusalem (Luke 9:51), ending with Jesus restoring to the servant of the high priest his right ear cut off by a disciple of Jesus in Gethsemane (22:51). In one way or another, all serve the purpose of the mission of Jesus.

6

JESUS THE GALILEAN

Birth and Early Years of Jesus the Galilean

The birth narratives of John and Jesus are parallel in structure and closely linked chronologically. After his service in the temple, Zechariah went home, Elizabeth became pregnant, and she remained in seclusion for the first five of the nine months of her pregnancy, no doubt on account of her advanced years. Then, at the beginning of the sixth month, Gabriel was sent on a second mission, this time to Mary (Miriam) in the small town of Nazareth in Galilee to announce that she too was to give birth to a child (Luke 1:26). Later in the same month, Mary, betrothed to a man called Joseph, who was of Davidic descent, undertook the long journey to Judaea to be with her pregnant relative and stayed with her for three months. We may assume that she stayed until Elizabeth gave birth, in spite of the impression given by the order of events in 1:56–57, dictated no doubt by the need to connect the birth of John with the congratulations of relatives and neighbors.

Gabriel's two visits are closely parallel. Both elicit fear and alarm (Luke 1:20; 1:29), both recipients of his messages are told not to be afraid (1:13; 1:30), and both announce the birth of a special child who will be great and whose name is given in advance (1:13–17; 1:30–33). Misgivings are expressed: Zechariah and Elizabeth are too old (1:18), Mary is a virgin betrothed to Joseph, and sexual relations are forbidden during the year preceding marriage (1:34).[1] In his reply to Zechariah, Gabriel reminds him that his mission is from God, and in punishment for his incredulity, he is temporarily deprived of speech (1:19–20). Gabriel's reply to Mary's misgivings is more enigmatic and, as the history of interpretation shows, can be understood in different ways. Few emerge unscathed from interpreting Luke 1:36, but the following paraphrase may nevertheless be hazarded: "The Holy Spirit will come upon you and the power of the Most High will overshadow you, as the male comes upon and overshadows the female in intercourse, so that the Holy One to be born will be called and will really be the son of God; God will be the child's father."

The name of the child to be born has already been given, and he has already been identified as "Son of the Most High" (Luke 1:31–32). Gabriel's reply is therefore a further clarification in response to Mary's troubled question about her present condition.

As we read on through the Gospel, we note how each event in the life of Jesus is presented as the fulfillment of prophecy. Mary, a virgin, will conceive and give birth to a son and call him Jesus (Luke 1:31), which is an adaptation of Isaiah 7:14: "a young woman shall conceive and bear a son, and shall call his name Imman'u-el," which means "God is with us." The statement about the child that follows in Luke 1:32–33 ("He will be great, and will be called the Son of the Most High; and the Lord God will give to him the throne of his father David . . . and of his kingdom there will be no end") is meant to recall Isaiah 9:6–7: "Of peace there will be no end, upon the throne of David, and over his kingdom, to establish it, and to uphold it with justice and with righteousness from this time forth and forevermore." This is therefore the birth of the Messiah, descendant of David (Isa 11:4; 29:19; 61:1). While yet in the womb he will be greeted by Elizabeth as "my Lord" (Luke 1:43; cf. Ps 110:1), the lord whose coming will be prepared for by Elizabeth's son, who will go before him in the spirit and power of the prophet Elijah (Luke 1:16–17; Isa 41:8–9; 49:13; 66:2).

The Magnificat (Luke 1:46–55)

The Magnificat—the well-known prayer of praise and thanksgiving—should be noted here, since it previews major characteristics of Luke's theology and moral teaching. At intervals in Luke's account of the birth and infancy of John and Jesus, the leading characters break into song or verse to praise God for the events that they have been privileged to witness: first Mary, Jesus's mother, for the birth of Jesus (Luke 1:46–55); then the priest Zechariah for the birth of John (1:67–79); and finally, Simeon, a holy man and visionary, one of several prophets who practically lived in the Jerusalem temple, in gratitude for seeing the beginning of redemption before dying (2:29–32). These canticles were probably taken over by Luke from the psalmody of a Judaic-Christian circle with a strong messianic orientation, probably the group associated with James in Jerusalem, whose members came to be known as "the poor" (Greek: *ptōchoi*; Hebrew: *'ănāwîm*) and were indeed poor enough to need support from the other churches (Rom 15:26; Gal 2:10). The broader understanding of "the poor," with reference to the alternative community God is gathering in every age, derives from the prophetic-eschatological language of Isaiah about the community of the future Zion. The primary reference of these three canticles, however, is to the situation of Israel in relation to the great powers throughout history—hence the frequent reference to God bringing down potentates from their thrones (Luke 1:52), setting his people free from their enemies (1:68–71), and doing so in the sight of all nations (2:31). Luke has adapted this language to the situation of the participants in the births of John and Jesus: Elizabeth, mother of John; Mary, mother of Jesus; Zechariah the priest; and Simeon the prophet and seer.

The Magnificat owes a debt to the canonical psalms of praise (e.g., Ps 149) and to the Isaian theme of Israel as Servant of the Lord. In addition, it has been modeled on the Septuagint version of the Song of Hannah, wife of Elkanah (1 Sam 2:1–10), especially where Hannah's psalm of praise expresses the theme of reversal between those of high and those of low status, between the wealthy who have plenty to eat and the poor who go hungry, and for good measure—since Hannah had just given birth to a child—between the woman with many children and the infertile woman (2:4–5). Hannah's hymn of thanksgiving and praise reads as follows:

> *The Lord metes out both death and life:*
> *he sends down to Sheol, he can bring the dead up again.*
> *Poverty and riches both come from the Lord;*
> *he brings low and he raises up.*
> *He lifts the weak out of the dust*
> *and raises the poor from the refuse heap*
> *to give them a place among the great,*
> *to assign them seats of honor. (1 Sam 2:6–8 REB)*

The reversal theme in the Magnificat is similar. The Lord who has looked with favor on the low status of Mary, his maidservant, has also brought down potentates from their thrones and raised on high the lowly; he has filled the hungry with good things and sent the rich away empty (Luke 1:52–53). We shall see that the parable of the rich man and Lazarus in chapter sixteen may be read as a dramatic illustration of this statement. The rich man is dressed in royal apparel like the potentates in the Magnificat but has been brought down to Sheol (or Hades), while Lazarus has been taken up by angels to be with Abraham. Lazarus is filled with good things (*ta agatha*, 16:25; cf. 1:53) at Abraham's table, like the hungry in the canticle, while the rich man has been sent away empty. In the third canticle, Simeon, after awaiting the consolation (*paraklēsis*) of Israel (2:25), is finally consoled, just as Lazarus has his consolation (*parakaleitai*, 16:25) after a lifetime of suffering.

This reversal theme, exploited throughout Luke's Gospel, was familiar in early Judaic-Christian circles. It appears in very succinct form toward the beginning of the circular letter ascribed to James, brother of Jesus, addressed to Christian communities scattered throughout the Middle East: "Let the lowly brother boast in his exaltation, and the rich in his humiliation, because like the flower of the grass he will pass away" (Jas 1:9–10).

We note finally that there is little overt moralizing in the canticle. Mary claims nothing for herself except her lowly station, but she now knows herself to be one of those on whom God looks with favor, as Isaiah had foretold: "This is the man to whom I will look, he that is humble and contrite in spirit, and trembles at my word" (Isa 66:2). A connection among pride, self-sufficiency, and the acquisition of great wealth is hinted at here (Luke 1:51b), but the main point in the canticle is the simple juxtaposition of rich with poor, well fed with hungry. This provides another hint that throughout Luke's Gospel, morality is essentially relational. Hence, in regard to wealth and poverty, it is precisely at this point, the coexistence of great wealth and great poverty, that the moral issue is located.

Luke's Version of the Birth Story (Luke 2:1–20)

Our social and traditional habits make it easy to forget that Christmas is the Feast of the Incarnation when, as Christians believe, God entered history in the person of Jesus—hence the importance of the historical dimension in general and the historical character of the Gospel narrative in particular, which, however, does not exclude the possibility of error in peripheral matters. We encounter an example of such an error at the beginning of the story of Jesus's birth with the relocation of Joseph and his pregnant wife from Nazareth in Galilee to Bethlehem just south of Jerusalem, normally a three-day journey. Luke explains this by reference to an edict issued by the Roman emperor Augustus (27 BCE–14 CE) mandating a census to be held throughout the empire for the purpose of assessing property and rates of taxation. Luke has it that this edict was implemented in Galilee by Quirinius, governor of the province of Syria, at a time when Herod, king of Judaea, was still alive (Luke 1:5; 2:1–7). According to Josephus, however, this census took place thirty-seven years after the decisive defeat of Anthony at the battle of Actium in 31 BCE—therefore in 6 CE (*Ant* 18:26).[2] Herod, active at the time Jesus was born, died in 4 BCE, so Jesus must have been born before 4 BCE. As noted earlier, we owe our distinction between BCE and CE to a calculation that was off by a few years.

In addition, there is considerable doubt about the requirement of returning to one's family place of origin, especially when accompanied by a pregnant wife, and the Gospels leave no doubt that Nazareth in Galilee was the original home of Joseph, Mary, and Jesus.[3] At this point, Luke is probably following a tradition in some early Christian communities of the birth of Jesus in Bethlehem, a tradition also taken over by Matthew (2:1). The reason for the relocation is the need to fulfill the Scriptures—in this instance, the prophet Micah 5:1 (Eng. Tr. 5:2):

> *You, Bethlehem of Ephratah, one of the little clans of Judah,*
> *from you will come a king for me to rule in Israel,*
> *whose origin is from old, from ancient days.*

The actual circumstances of the birth are well known. Since there were no vacancies at the local lodging place, Joseph and Mary had to make do with a cattle shed, perhaps attached to the aforesaid lodging place, and their first visitors were shepherds who were guided there by angels—the first of many instances of the inversion of status and value in social life, which is one of the prominent features of Luke's Gospel. This contrasts with the account in Matthew's Gospel, in which the magi (professional astronomers and members of the intellectual elite wherever they came from) pay homage to Jesus in a house (Matt 2:11).

The First Twelve Years (Luke 2:21–52)

In keeping with the law (Lev 12:3), Jesus was circumcised on the eighth day, and as with John, the name-giving had been anticipated by angelic message (Luke 1:31). Luke, perhaps not well informed about Palestinian Judaic practice, conflates the presentation of Jesus in the temple, also prescribed by the law (Exod 13:2, 11–16; Num 18:15), with the rite of purification of the mother thirty-three days after giving birth—sixty-six days if the child is a female. Mary would then have made an offering of two turtledoves or two pigeons (Lev 12:1–8). This visit to the temple led to an encounter with Simeon, a visionary who recognized the child Jesus as the future Messiah and uttered a short hymn of thanksgiving, and with Anna, an octogenarian prophetess, who was also waiting and praying in the temple for the redemption of Jerusalem at the coming of the Messiah (Luke 2:25–38).

These dramatic events are then summarized. The parents, having fulfilled all requirements of the law of God, returned to Galilee and Nazareth (Luke 2:39). As the child continued to grow and become strong, he was full of wisdom and enjoyed the favor of God (2:40). The parallel with the conclusion to the childhood of John is unmistakable: "The child grew and became strong in spirit, and he was in the wilderness till the day of his manifestation to Israel" (1:80). Both echo the conclusion to the childhood of the prophet Samuel, son of Elkanah and Hannah: "The boy Samuel continued to grow both in stature and in favor with the Lord and with men" (1 Sam 2:26).[4]

The gap between this earliest phase in the life of Jesus and his parents' discovery of the twelve-year-old adolescent Jesus in the temple (Luke 2:41–50) called for another similar conclusion: "He went down with them and came to Nazareth, and was obedient to them. . . . And Jesus increased in wisdom and in stature, and in favor with God and man" (2:51). This interval between the infant Jesus presented in the temple and the adolescent Jesus discovered in the temple discoursing with the learned is filled in by those apocryphal writers who give their imaginations free rein on these missing years in the life of Jesus.[5] For example, the schoolboy Jesus becomes the teacher rather than the pupil. He works a wide range of miracles, including punitive miracles, among them making birds out of clay, which flew away at his command; raising a boy from the dead who had fallen off a roof; healing a companion bitten by a viper; and striking another boy dead for pushing him. Such fanciful episodes may be entertaining, but none of them adds anything of substance to our knowledge of the life of Jesus.

Galilee, Jesus's Home Ground

Family has an important role in determining attitudes toward wealth and poverty, the wealthy and the poor, but location and social milieu are also significant factors. Jesus, known by many as Jesus of Nazareth, was a Galilean and spent most of his relatively short life in Galilee. In spite of its name—originally *galil haggoyim* (district of the gentiles)—Galilee was still thoroughly Judaic at the time of Jesus, though given low marks for Torah observance by early Tannaitic rabbis.[6] It was ruled on behalf of the Roman overlords by Herod Antipas from the death of his father, Herod the Great, in 4 BCE to his own deposition and exile in 39 CE. Antipas rebuilt Sepphoris, close to Nazareth, and founded Tiberias on the Sea of Galilee in honor of the new emperor in 14 CE. These cities, and other less prominent towns and villages, could draw on an agrarian economy in a particularly fertile part of Palestine. As always, however, there were problems: the uncertainties of weather and occasional drought and famine; poverty exacerbated by taxation, including payment of the annual tribute levied by the Romans and the temple tax; the frequent enclosure of peasant holdings by the large estates, often for inability to repay loans; and other depredations of the ruling pro-Roman class.[7]

There was also social unrest of the kind that would lead to revolt against the Roman overlords and, in 66 CE, the war of independence, which ended with the destruction of the Jerusalem temple. Josephus records much unrest in Galilee during the lifetime of Jesus, no doubt also instigated by the census mandated by Rome with the purpose of assessing property subject to taxation. The most dangerous and persistent of the "disturbers of the peace" was Judah the Galilean, though according to Josephus, he came from Gamala, east of the Jordan. Writing under the patronage of imperial Rome, Josephus comments that this Judah and his followers "sowed the seed of every kind of misery" (*Ant* 18 §6), and his sons continued sowing the same seeds in the years leading to the war of independence. Two sons, James and Simon, were arrested and crucified (*Ant* 20 §102); a third son, Menahem, was assassinated by a rival faction (*JW* 2 §447–48); and yet another descendant, Eleazar, led the final resistance to Rome on the rock of Masada (Josephus, *Judaic War* 2 §447; 7 §252–53).

Jesus Returns to Nazareth (Luke 4:14–30)

After the high drama in the wilderness in confrontation with Satan, Jesus returned to Galilee, where he was brought up. Galilee was Jesus's home ground, and his first stop was in Nazareth (4:16–30). This is not the place for a detailed account of this visit, which ended badly, but it is relevant to our theme to note that Jesus, invited by the president of the synagogue to read the lesson for the day from the prophets (the *haftarah*) and preach on it, made use of the occasion, and Isaiah 61:1–2 (REB) proclaims his mission statement. The text begins as follows:

> *The spirit of the Lord is upon me*
> *because the Lord has anointed me;*
> *he has sent me to announce good news to the poor,*
> *to proclaim liberty to captives,*
> *release to those in prison.*

In Isaiah and Psalms, "the poor" (Hebrew: *'ănāwîm*) is a title that, together with "the servants of the Lord," refers to the faithful remnant, the alternative community, the core of a renewed and purified people that God was gathering then and gathers at all times. It testifies to the importance for Luke of the poverty-wealth theme that this *sensus plenior* (fuller sense) of the term *poor* is taken from Isaiah and Psalms at the same time it is addressed to the poor present and visible—that is, those deprived of the means for living a decent and productive life. As Jesus uses the term, these poor include the blind, the deaf, and in general, the disabled; they also consist of those unjustly detained and imprisoned and those suffering oppression, including oppression by illness or other misfortunes. Luke's reasonable assumption is that all of these qualify as "the poor," and all are the object of Jesus's care and benevolence (Isa 11:4; 29:19; 61:1; Pss 25:9; 37:11; 69:33; 76:10; 147:6; 149:4).

Unlike John's mission as a herald of the impending judgment—the time of wrath, the ax laid at the roots of the trees, and the like (Luke 3:7–9)—in the sermon preached in the Nazareth synagogue, Jesus states his mission in entirely positive terms, with special emphasis on the poor and needy. It will be repeated in the incident, mentioned earlier, in which John sends two of his followers to inquire of Jesus whether he is the one "who is to come" (7:18–23). This is not the place to discuss the many explanations of John's question and the answer that it received beginning in the patristic period, but if "the One to Come" refers to the messenger of Malachi 3:1, an Elijah figure who will prepare the way for the coming of God in judgment (Mal 3:23–24; Eng. Trans. 4:5–6), the reply of Jesus to John's messengers presents John with a very different understanding of the mission of Jesus: "Go and tell John what you have seen and heard: the blind receive their sight, the lame walk, lepers are cleansed, and the deaf hear, the dead are raised up, the poor have good news preached to them" (Luke 7:22). In effect, this reply of Jesus repeats the message proclaimed in the Nazareth synagogue. Both are based on Isaiah's vision of the future directed toward the most indigent and disadvantaged in society: the poor and, among them, the blind, the lame, the deaf, and those afflicted with leprosy, including disfiguring skin diseases, which resulted in temporary or permanent exclusion from society. On this showing, salvation consists for Jesus, in the first instance, of removing obstacles for people to live normal, active, and productive lives. His message is that God has made up his mind on behalf of the poor.

Jesus in Capernaum (Luke 4:39–44)

The visit to Nazareth ended in a riot when some of those present complained about Jesus's failure to heal and work miracles for them, and Jesus, undaunted, replied by comparing them unfavorably to gentiles in Sidon and Syria, which, in turn, led to an attempted lynching. Why Jesus then decided to move to Capernaum, a short distance north of Tiberias on the Sea of Galilee (Kinnereth), we are not told, but since some of the worshippers in Nazareth had heard of his remarkable deeds in that town (Luke 4:23), it may have been simply a return to a place more receptive to his message. Capernaum—there are several variations of spelling[8]—was one of several prosperous settlements in the Plain of Gennesaret closed in between hills to the west and the Sea of Galilee to the east. Well known for its fruit trees, barley, and wheat, this region was especially famous for the salting and export of fish. Tarichaea (Magdala), the presumed place of origin of Mary Magdalen, was one of the leading centers for this industry, well known throughout the east and as far away as Rome. In addition, archaeological excavations attest to the existence of several related installations along the shore of the Sea of Tiberias.[9] This information may suggest a somewhat more nuanced perspective on the disciples whom Jesus conscripted from this region, often taken to be poor and probably uneducated and illiterate, eking out a bare subsistence by fishing.[10]

We learned from the dispute in the Nazareth synagogue that this was not Jesus's first visit to Capernaum (Luke 4:23), and we now gather that he was already acquainted with Simon, since he went directly from the synagogue to his house, where he healed his mother-in-law. The house seems to have served as a gathering point for those seeking relief from illnesses of different kinds, especially leprosy, which implied separation from society, and freedom from demonic possession in keeping with the mission announced in the Nazareth synagogue to bring the good news of the kingdom to the poor, prisoners, the blind, and others similarly afflicted.

Examples of the Mission of Jesus

After the calling to discipleship of Simon, together with James and John, sons of Zebedee and Simon's coworkers in the fishing business (Luke 5:1–11), Luke presents, in no particular chronological sequence, examples of how Jesus carried out his mission of making the kingdom of God a reality on earth (5:12–32; 6:1–11). What is common to these examples is illustrated by a discussion between Jesus and certain Pharisees and scribes whom Jesus had scandalized by accepting an invitation to dine with Levi and other tax collectors (5:33–39). They want to know why Pharisees and the followers of John lead an ascetic life with frequent fasts while Jesus and his followers—not many at that point—do not. He replies that they do not fast because the bridegroom—God's representative—is still with them. The first example, also in Matthew 8:1–4 and Mark 1:40–45 with variations, is the healing of a man suffering from leprosy, a term (Hebrew: *sora'at*) that included a broad range of disfiguring skin conditions requiring segregation from society, perhaps for life. The rules and procedures for treatment and certification of cure by a priest are laid out in great detail in the ritual law. Noteworthy is Jesus's insistence that the one healed submit to the certification process and thus qualify to reenter society.

A second example of healing involves a successful attempt by some men to get their paralyzed friend, who is lying inert on a pallet, into the presence of Jesus, at that moment in a house crowded with people, by way of the roof (Luke 5:17–26).[11] Jesus acknowledges their heroic effort and takes the occasion to provoke an argument with Pharisees and lawyers who happened to be present by assuring the sick man that his sins are forgiven, in confirmation of which he heals him, saying, "Get up, pick up your pallet, and go home," and to everyone's astonishment, he does so.

In the remaining three examples, it is clear that for Jesus, the ritual law gives place to human needs. In the first (Luke 5:27–32), in which Jesus recruits a tax collector or customs officer as a disciple and accepts an invitation to a goodbye banquet with Levi and his colleagues, Jesus ignores the prohibition against commensality with such people. Both remaining examples deal with a purely technical violation of Sabbath law about work: the first, pulling and chewing ears of corn when passing through a cornfield (6:1–5), and the second, healing a man with a withered arm during the Sabbath service (6:6–11). For Jesus, however, "The sabbath was made for man, not man for the sabbath" (Mark 2:27).

7

JESUS THE TEACHER

Jesus the Teacher in Luke's Gospel

Referring back to the first of the two volumes, the Acts of the Apostles describes Luke's Gospel as an account of what Jesus did and taught from the beginning to the day when he departed from them (Acts 1:1–3). Throughout the Gospel of Luke, the teaching of Jesus takes place in different locations and is addressed to different individuals and groups: sometimes to the crowds that followed him on his peripatetic mission in Galilee and Judaea, sometimes to the disciples he had chosen. It was as teacher (*didaskalos*) that he was addressed and acknowledged by the public (Luke 9:38; 12:13; 21:7) and by members of elite groups like Pharisees (7:40; 19:39), Sadducees (20:28), revenue officers (3:12), and the ruling class (18:18) and also by scribes (20:21, 39) and lawyers (10:25; 11:45). The principal concern of scribes and lawyers was the study and interpretation of *tôrāh* (hereafter *torah*), a term that can refer either to collections of laws in the Pentateuch or to the Pentateuch in general as a guide to the moral life, usually in the form "the Law and the Prophets." The preferred venue for addressing the public was the local synagogue, and Jesus made good use of this place of public assembly for teaching and spreading his message (4:15, 44), beginning with the synagogues in Nazareth (4:16) and

Capernaum (4:33; 7:5; e.g., Luke 19:47–48). We have seen that it was in the Nazareth synagogue that Jesus first announced his mission on behalf of the poor, disabled, and oppressed in a sermon based on his reading of Isaiah 61:1–2. After making the decision to go to Jerusalem (9:51)—the *peripateia*, or turning point, in the Gospel of Luke—and completing the journey in stages to this city of destiny, the temple became the venue of choice for addressing the public. As long as the temple stood, it continued to be for his disciples in Jerusalem the proper place for prayer and proclaiming the good news.[1]

The Sermon on the Plain

After a series of more or less hostile encounters with Pharisees and scribes, who appear to have been following Jesus around (Luke 5:17–6:11), it was time to be alone and spend the night in prayer on a mountain (6:12). At daybreak, he selected the Twelve who were to form the leaders among his disciples, the ones with a special mission who were therefore also known as apostles (6:12–16). Three of these—Simon Peter, James, and John—had already been recruited as disciples by the Sea of Galilee (5:1–11), and the same three would form the inner circle of the group, the only ones who would witness the transfiguration of Jesus during prayer, perhaps on the same mountain (9:28–36). The number twelve signified that these disciples represented Israel as a twelve-tribe entity, but Luke will later introduce another seventy-two disciples corresponding to the seventy-two nations of the world (10:1–12).[2] Their mission signified the definitively universal reach of the Jesus movement.

After the commissioning of the Twelve, Jesus came down with them to a level place and was at once surrounded by a great crowd from Jerusalem and Judaea to the south and the maritime cities of Tyre and Sidon to the north, and no doubt places in between. They assembled there to hear Jesus, some bringing with them their sick or demented relatives, friends, and acquaintances in the hope of a cure

(Luke 6:17–19). There follows what has come to be known as the "Sermon on the Plain," the Lukan parallel to Matthew's much longer "Sermon on the Mount" (Matt 5:1–7:29). Reading the two versions together will help us grasp what is unique in the Lukan version.

This "Sermon on the Plain" (Luke 6:17–49) is manifestly not a transcript of what Jesus said on one particular occasion. It is a composite put together by the author drawing on material about Jesus passed on by those "servants of the word," contemporaries of Jesus mentioned in his prologue. The account of the call to discipleship of the Twelve in the Gospel of Mark also takes place on a mountain, with a great multitude from even farther afield than in Luke's version waiting below for contact and healing with Jesus (Mark 3:13–19). In the Matthean version, Jesus goes up the mountain to get away from the crowd and his disciples follow him, giving the impression that the entire "sermon" takes place on the mountain and is heard only by his disciples (Matt 5:1–2). Notwithstanding this location, we are told at the conclusion of the discourse that the crowd was amazed by his teaching (7:28–29). The "level place" where Jesus speaks in Luke may simply be a way of marking the appropriate place for Jesus to interact with the public, in contrast with the mountain reserved for his disciples. Mountains have a special place in Luke's Gospel: think of the mountain on which Jesus was transfigured in prayer, mentioned earlier (Luke 9:28–36), and the Mount of Olives, also a place of revelation, toward the end of the story (19:37; 22:39).

The components that make up Luke's "Sermon on the Plain" are easily identified:

1. The beatitudes and woes (6:20–26)
2. The command to love enemies (6:27–36)
3. Admonitions about conduct in a community of disciples (27–42)
4. Conclusion (43–49)

1. The Beatitudes and Woes (Luke 6:20–26)

First, the beatitudes and woes are addressed to all, including the disciples, who have now come down from the mountain with Jesus:

> Blessed are you poor, for yours is the kingdom of God.
>
> Blessed are you that hunger now, for you shall be satisfied.
>
> Blessed are you that weep now, for you shall laugh.
>
> Blessed are you when men hate you, and when they exclude you and revile you, and cast out your name as evil, on account of the Son of man! Rejoice in that day, and leap for joy, for behold, your reward is great in heaven; for so their fathers did to the prophets. (Luke 6:20–23)

Comparison of Luke's beatitudes with those of Matthew (5:1–12) will help us understand and appreciate what Luke has to say elsewhere in the Gospel about the poor and the rich, poverty and wealth, including the parable of the rich man and Lazarus (Luke 16:19–31). In the first place, the Matthean version spiritualizes what in Luke is stated and intended literally: in Matthew, the blessed poor are the poor in spirit and the hungry are those who hunger after justice, whereas in Luke, the poor are literally poor and the hungry are literally hungry, like Lazarus.[3] Luke may have had in mind the early Judaic-Christian community in Jerusalem after Jesus had departed. They were known as "the poor" (Greek: *ptōchoi*; Hebrew: *'ănāwîm*) in the sense in which the term is used in Isaiah and Psalms, referring to the alternative society that God gathers in all ages, but they were also literally poor and in need of assistance from other churches (Acts 11:29; Rom 15:25–27; Gal 2:9–10). The most significant difference, however, is the addition in Luke of a series of four woes corresponding to the four beatitudes: a woe on the wealthy in antithesis to the poor, on the well fed in antithesis to the hungry, on those who rejoice and are at ease in antithesis to those who are now mourning, and on the well regarded, the socially acceptable, over against those now despised and excluded:

But woe to you that are rich, for you have received your consolation.
Woe to you that are full now, for you shall hunger.
Woe to you that laugh now, for you shall mourn and weep.
Woe to you, when all men speak well of you, for so their fathers did to the false prophets. (6:24–26)

These antitheses correspond to one of the most dominant themes in Luke's Gospel. They are exemplified in the Magnificat by the contrast between the fate of the powerful of this world and that of the lowly and between the fate of the wealthy, who have the means to eat well, and those who go hungry for lack of means (Luke 1:52–53). Yet clearer is the contrast between the wealthy, who have had their consolation (6:24), and the poor, for whom the kingdom of God awaits (6:23). These correspond, as we shall see, to the contrasting fates of the anonymous rich man of the parable, who had good things during his lifetime, and Lazarus, who, after a life of poverty, hunger, and sickness, is now consoled (16:25).

2. The Command to Love Enemies (Luke 6:27–36)

Second, the command to love enemies (Luke 6:27–36) is also addressed both to disciples and to those who had come from far and near to hear Jesus. This section is easily identified by this injunction placed at its beginning and end (6:27, 35). To it Luke has added another command: "Be merciful, even as your Father is merciful" (6:36). This is a modified form of Matthew's conclusion to the Sermon on the Mount: "Be perfect, as your heavenly Father is perfect" (Matt 5:48), which Luke may have found too demanding and unrealistic. This segment illustrates the counterintuitive character of the preaching of Jesus noted earlier, a feature that is surely authentic. There is also an element of deliberate hyperbole here, as there is throughout Luke's Gospel: for example, taking the speck out of your brother's eye while not seeing the plank in your own eye (Luke

6:41), the camel passing through the eye of a needle (18:25), and other sayings of this kind. At the beginning and end of this address to the public and the disciples, the imperative is love of enemies:

> Love your enemies, do good to those who hate you. (Luke 6:27)
>
> Love your enemies, and do good to them. (6:35)

In the original Greek, as in other languages, "love" takes on many forms. The kind of love called for here is not *philia*, the warm kind that generally exists between members of a family or close friends, and much less is it *eros*, that between lovers and spouses. The verb used here is *agapaō* (substantive: *agapē*), indicating an emotion that leads one to have a regard for and interest in the well-being of others even when these sentiments are not reciprocated or are rejected. Examples of the exercise of this *agapē* follow: "From him who takes away your coat do not withhold even your shirt" (Luke 6:29).

This goes beyond John's advice to those who came to be baptized that whoever has two coats must share with one who has none and whoever has food must do likewise (Luke 3:11). These and the following injunctions are illustrative of the radical demands placed on the disciples of Jesus, members of the alternative community that Jesus is gathering. Those demands will often be incomprehensible to those outside. They are formulated in Luke's typically totalizing language. He is saying with Paul, with whom he was probably associated, "Do not be conformed to this world but be transformed by the renewal of your mind, that you may prove what is the will of God, what is good and acceptable and perfect" (Rom 12:2):

> Give to every one who begs from you. (Luke 6:30)
>
> Of him who takes away your goods do not ask them again. (6:30)
>
> As you wish that men would do to you, do so to them. (6:31)

> Lend, expecting nothing in return. (6:35)
>
> Be merciful, even as your Father is merciful. (6:36)[4]

To these exhortations is attached a promise:

> In whatever measure you give, it will be given to you in return. (6:38, my paraphrase)

3. Admonitions about Conduct in a Community of Disciples (Luke 6:27–42)

Third are the admonitions about conduct in a community of disciples (Luke 6:37–42). This advice must have been directed in the first place to the disciples present and, through them, to the churches known to Luke. The need to avoid passing sanctimonious judgment on others, to forgive injuries and slights, to follow approved teachers who will not mislead (the blind leading the blind), and to learn from such teachers before aspiring to leadership—all of this suggests reference to early Christian communities, beginning with the earliest established in Jerusalem under the leadership of Simon Peter and James. One of the clearest indications of this intent is the use of the language of brotherhood common in early Christian circles (Luke 6:41–42; also Acts 1:15–16; 6:3; 1 Cor 1:1; 2 Cor 1:1; etc.). Everything we know about early Christian communities from the Acts of the Apostles, the Pauline letters, and other early Christian writings confirms the origin of these counsels in church life, the everyday life in early Christian communities.

4. Conclusion (Luke 6:43–49)

Finally, the conclusion to the teaching (Luke 6:43–49) presents the figure of the good fruit tree, necessary for the production of good fruit (6:43–45; cf. Matt 7:16–20). This is followed by an insistence on not just listening to what is said but putting the teaching into practice, using the metaphor of building a house on firm foundations (Luke 6:47–49). The repetition "Lord, Lord" (*kurie, kurie*), borrowed from Matthew 7:21 or from a source common to both, may have been directed against certain charismatic groups in some of the churches that practiced ecstatic and repetitive prayer, perhaps influenced by contemporary Greek cults, while remaining indifferent to the needs of others. Much of this final section is borrowed from the conclusion to Matthew's Sermon on the Mount (Matt 7:21–27).

The Law in Luke's Gospel

It may seem strange that this "Sermon on the Plain" contains no exhortation to observe the Law, or indeed any mention of the Law (*torah, nomos*), in any of its several formulations and contexts. In Gospel usage, the term *torah* has three principal references:

- a procedure or practice that has taken hold
- a constitutional or statutory legal system
- a collection of holy writings, Scripture[5]

An example of the first would be circumcision. Though circumcision is also prescribed in the Law, its practice is more often traced back to father Abraham, who circumcised himself when he was ninety-nine years old and Ishmael was thirteen (Gen 17:24–26). Some Judaic believers associated with James, brother of the Lord, insisted that unless gentile converts were circumcised according to the custom established by Moses, they could not be saved (Acts 15:4–5). The second reference includes the Decalogue (Exod 20:1–17; Deut 5:6–21), the covenant code (Exod 20:22–23:33), and other legal enactments in Exodus and Deuteronomy together with ritual rules and procedures in Leviticus and Numbers.

The third, usually in the form "the Law and the Prophets," is more or less identical to sacred Scripture. The most obvious explanation for the absence of the law from the Sermon on the Plain would seem to be that observance of the law is simply taken for granted, as elsewhere in the Gospel. So, for example, the lawyer who asked Jesus what he must do to obtain eternal life was told to consult the law; he did so and came up with a combination of Deuteronomy 6:5 and Leviticus 19:18 (Luke 10:25–27).

In the parable of the rich man and Lazarus, the rich man in Hades begs father Abraham to send Lazarus, now reclining in Abraham's bosom, to his five brothers to warn them to change their conduct in order to avoid sharing the fate of their brother. They receive a curt reply: "They have Moses and the prophets; let them hear them" (Luke 16:29). The emphasis here is clearly on Moses as lawgiver.

Laws in Favor of the Poor

As noted earlier, ancient Hebrew has several terms for the poor, most of which occur in the laws. It is equally important to note that favorable treatment of the poor in the pentateuchal laws also applies as a matter of course to related categories: in the first place to widows, orphans, and resident aliens, this last of which is comparable to immigrants in our world, whose need for just and compassionate treatment according to the laws of the countries in which they aspire to settle is evident.

The pentateuchal laws governing the poor are of different kinds and presuppose a broad range of situations. These laws insist on the right to the same just treatment for resident aliens as applies to residents (Exod 22:21–25; 23:9). The poor must not be exploited in courts of law—for example, by false charges or the demand for a bribe (23:6–8). Likewise, interest must not be required when granting a loan (22:25). If a garment is taken in pledge from a poor person, it must be returned by sunset, since the poor often sleep in the open in their outer garments (Deut 24:17). The prophet Amos mentions a particularly heinous violation of these injunctions, perhaps involving temple clergy:

> *They lay themselves down beside every altar*
> *upon garments taken in pledge;*
> *and in the house of their God they drink*
> *the wine of those who have been fined. (Amos 2:8)*

The laws also insist that workers be paid their wages by sunset each day because their livelihood could be at stake (Deut 24:14–15; cf. Luke 3:11).

These demands are reformulated in Luke's typically totalizing language. He says with Paul, with whom he was closely associated, "Do not be conformed to this world but be transformed by the renewal of your mind, that you may prove what is the will of God, what is good and acceptable and perfect" (Rom 12:2). In different places, Paul's Letter to the Romans is behind the following imperatives in Luke's teaching:

> Give to every one who begs from you. (Luke 6:30)
>
> As you wish that men would do to you, do so to them. (6:31)
>
> Lend without expecting any return. (6:34, my translation)
>
> Be merciful, even as your Father is merciful. (6:36)

To these is added a promise:

> In whatever measure you give, it will be given to you in return. (6:38, my paraphrase)

The Three Phases of Salvation History in Luke's Gospel

To obtain a clearer idea of Luke's understanding of *torah* as a legal system or collection of laws set out in the Pentateuch—with the exception of Genesis, which is the only book of the five without laws—we begin with the concept of salvation history in Luke's Gospel. We can identify three phases of that history according to Luke.

The first is the time of the Law and the Prophets as predictive of the coming kingdom of God.

The second phase is the proclamation and initial implementation of the kingdom by Jesus and his disciples, beginning with the public appearance of Jesus after his baptism and the announcement of his mission in the Nazareth synagogue. This second phase ends not with the death and resurrection of Jesus but with his final departure from his followers on the Mount of Olives (Acts 1:6–11). The proclamation and implementation of the kingdom do not, however, exclude opposition and even persecution, intimated in Jesus's cryptic remark at his last meal with his disciples: "'When I sent you out with no purse or bag or sandals, did you lack anything?' They said, 'Nothing.' He said to them, 'But now, let him who has a purse take it, and likewise a bag. And let him who has no sword sell his mantle and buy one'" (Luke 22:35–36).

The third phase is the time when the good news begins to spread throughout the world. After the establishment of the first churches, it will nevertheless be a time of strife and persecution anticipated by Jesus (Luke 24:50–51; Acts 1:1–2, 9–11).[6]

The distinction between the first and second of these three phases is of special importance for Luke. Its clearest expression is in the three anticipatory comments on the parable of the rich man and Lazarus, to which we will return in due course. The first reads as follows: "The [period of] law and the prophets were until John; since then the good news of the kingdom of God is preached, and every one enters it violently" (Luke 16:16). That John the Baptist belongs to the first and not the second phase is clearly implied in another saying of Jesus: "I tell you, among those born of women none is greater than John; yet he who is least in the [period of the] kingdom of God is greater than he" (7:28; cf. Matt 11:11). John therefore belonged to the first epoch, that of the Law and the Prophets. However, the use of the term *torah* in Luke's first statement leaves room for ambiguity, as if *torah* understood as law also belonged to the first epoch and was therefore superseded. To dispel this conclusion, Luke adds a second comment: "It is easier for heaven and earth to pass away, than for one dot of the law (*torah*) to become void" (16:17).

Even more explicit is the fuller statement in Matthew's Gospel:

> Think not that I have come to abolish the law and the prophets; I have come not to abolish them but to fulfil them. For truly, I say to you, till heaven and earth pass away, not an iota, not a dot, will pass from the law until all is accomplished. Whoever then relaxes one of the least of these commandments and teaches men so, shall be called least in the kingdom of heaven; but he who does them and teaches them shall be called great in the kingdom of heaven. For I tell you, unless your righteousness exceeds that of the scribes and Pharisees, you will never enter the kingdom of heaven. (5:17–20)

Luke then adds an example of these laws: "Every one who divorces his wife and marries another commits adultery, and he who marries a woman divorced from her husband commits adultery" (16:18).[7] Why this particular example is given at this point, in what appears to be commentary on the parable of the rich man and Lazarus, has proved something of a puzzle for commentators on Luke's Gospel. It corresponds to Matthew 5:32 in the aforementioned Q source common to Matthew and Luke and may have been picked at random to make the point about the relevance of law, perhaps at an earlier stage in the development of all the sayings traditions. Of possible relevance is the insistence in the Epistle of James (attributed to James, brother of Jesus) against picking and choosing among the laws as if, for example, one were to observe the prohibition of adultery but not the prohibition against murder (Jas 2:8–11). But a different kind of explanation may be suggested based on the literary context of the saying. Since Luke 16:18 is a comment on the parable of the rich man and Lazarus, which follows immediately after it, it may be related to something in the parable. This option may be better discussed at a later stage, in connection with our reading of this parable.

In brief, with one exception, the incident in Luke in which the lawyer asks Jesus how to obtain eternal life and is referred to the first commandment of the Law (Luke 10:25–29), allusion to the Law (Greek: *nomos*) with the meaning of a constitutional or statutory legal system is confined to the accounts of the birth and infancy of John and Jesus. Jesus accepts the Law, but his new message about the kingdom of God goes beyond it.[8]

The Background: Luke's Second Volume

Since Luke's Gospel reaches out to the world beyond Judaism, most explicitly in the mission of the Seventy-Two (Luke 10:1–12), it would be helpful to take account, if only briefly, of his second volume, which describes the long and often contentious process by which the Christian movement detached itself from the world within which it came into existence and in which it functioned for a time as a movement or sect. This is a subject too broad and complex to pursue here, but one instance may be cited. Paul, brought before Felix the governor on a charge of disturbing the peace and profaning the temple, was accused of being a ringleader of the sect of the Nazarenes. Paul rejected this description of himself and his fellow disciples of Jesus as a sect (Greek: *hairesis*). He insisted instead on using the title "The Way" (Acts 24:5–14), which had the advantage of avoiding the often negative implications of the term *hairesis* while at the same time signifying for believers the way of salvation opened to them by God through Jesus (Acts 18:25–26; 19:9–23). This was in fulfillment of a well-known prophecy:

> *A voice cries:*
> *"In the wilderness prepare the way of the Lord,*
> *Make straight in the desert a highway for our God." (Isa 40:3–4)*[9]

This title, the Way (*ha-derek* in Hebrew; *hodos* in Greek), remained in common use among the early followers of Jesus and his way of life. While it may still be used to remind us of a way of living, which is in many respects different from "the way of the world," it was replaced by the title "Christian" for the first time in Antioch, one of the great centers of early Christianity.

8

JESUS THE STORYTELLER

Four Parables

It is often said, and it may be true, that we learn more life lessons by listening to or reading stories than from written laws, precepts, or well-meaning admonitions. In the Gospels, the stories are known as parables, and as we read on in Luke's Gospel, we can test the truth of the claim that we learn more from parables than from other forms of teaching. We will probably also end up agreeing that among Gospel parables, those of Luke are the best.

But first, what is a parable? In the broadest terms, parable is a genre or literary type that makes use of comparison or analogy, of the same type as figurative language. The word itself derives from the Greek verb *paraballein*, meaning "to place one thing next to another"—in our case a type, figure, symbol, or brief narrative that points, often enigmatically, to a reality beyond itself. In the Gospels, not all cases of such juxtaposition are in narrative form. In Luke's Gospel, for example, the proverbial saying "Physician, heal yourself" (Luke 4:23) or reference to the blind leading the blind (6:39) are classed as parables, as are maxims warning against putting new patches on old garments or, the contrary, new wine in old wineskins (we are tempted to add "any kind of skin"), which, in the Gospels, serve to emphasize the newness of the presence and the message of Jesus (5:36–39).

We will therefore begin by distinguishing between aphoristic parables—that is, sayings in the form of proverbs, maxims, or allegories—from parables in narrative form. These are imaginative narratives that illuminate some aspect of the mission and teaching of Jesus and that invite interpretation as such. The difference between the aphoristic and narrative types is not always clear-cut. The story of the barren fig tree (Luke 13:6–9), for example, is called a parable. It is located within a residual, small-scale narrative about a man who planted the tree in a vineyard—which seems to have been a mistake to begin with—came looking for figs over a period of three years, and not finding any, ordered his servant to cut it down, but then he gave it one more year to produce some figs or fall victim to the ax.

Since we are concentrating on one record of the life and teaching of Jesus, the one presented in Luke's Gospel, we will confine ourselves to parables in that Gospel, each situated in its own context. We therefore omit the aphoristic parables and those with only a residual narrative character. This leaves us with the following six substantial narrative parables, all found only in Luke's Gospel.

Please note that in the list that follows, the references in parentheses refer to the text of the parable itself followed by its context in the Gospel.

The Grateful Debtors	7:41–43; 7:36–50
The Good Samaritan	10:30–35; 10:29–37
The Rich Fool	12:16–21; 12:13–31
The Son Lost and Found	15:11–32; 15:1–32
The Clever Steward	16:1–8; 16:1–15
The Rich Man and Lazarus	16:19–31; 16:16–31

A remarkable feature of these parables is that all six deal in one way or another with wealth and poverty, the rich and the poor, and also the use and abuse of money and possessions, a unique concern of this Gospel. The first parable is about lending and borrowing, the second is about using money to assist those in need, the third highlights the futility of the single-minded pursuit of wealth, the fourth is about inheriting wealth, the fifth commends the shrewd and productive use of personal wealth even when self-interested, and the last presents a moral paradigm about the coexistence of great wealth and great poverty, a situation still familiar in our own day.

We will undertake a reading of these six parables, paying due attention to the narrative context essential to understanding the purpose of Jesus in telling them and of Luke in narrating them in his Gospel. We will take the first through the fourth together as illustrative of different aspects of the subject. The fifth and the sixth, sharing the same context in chapter 16, call for a particularly close reading and will therefore claim our attention in the final chapter.

The Parable of the Grateful Debtors (Luke 7:41–42; 7:36–50)

This first of the six, brief and to the point, reads as follows: "A certain creditor had two debtors; one owed five hundred denarii, and the other fifty. When they could not pay, he forgave them both. Now which of them will love him more?" (Luke 7:41–42).[1] Concluding with a question suggests a riddle or puzzle rather than a parable, but the answer to the question is so obvious that it must have been posed by Jesus precisely to elicit the answer required by the remarkable incident in the house of Jesus's host, Simon the Pharisee. We shall see that this incident provides the occasion for the parable and the key to its interpretation. Given the reputation of money lenders, we may suspect here a suggestion of sly humor on the part of Jesus. Money lenders rarely seek love or expect to be loved. This is understandable. In wishing everything bad on his enemy, the author of Psalm 109 hopes that the creditor will seize all his enemy's possessions (Ps 109:11). For Sirach (Ecclesiasticus), a creditor is one of the two worst things for a decent person to tolerate (Sir 29:28). In any case, the question of which of two debtors—one owing fifty denarii or the other ten times as much—will have more love for (or at least positive feeling toward) the creditor who forgives both debts permits only one answer. We need hardly applaud Simon the Pharisee for getting it right.

The Incident in the House of Simon the Pharisee

The link between this brief parable and the narrative context in which it is situated is the idea of forgiveness—forgiveness of debt and forgiveness of sin. The same association is apparent in the Lord's Prayer in its original form, in which the one praying asks God to cancel our "debts" (Greek: *opheilēmata*)—that is, our sins—as we cancel the "debts" (i.e., the offenses) of those indebted to us (Matt 6:12), which is a more accurate and intelligible rendering than the translated form, "forgive us our trespasses as we forgive the trespasses of others." The situation that provided the occasion for the parable is Jesus's acceptance of an invitation to a meal from a Pharisee named Simon. In spite of the criticism of Pharisees collectively in the Gospels, Jesus had friendly relations with individual Pharisees; accepted invitations to share meals with them, as here and later in the Gospel (Luke 11:37–41); and was on first-name terms with some, as with Simon on this occasion. But as they were at the table, an extraordinary thing happened. A woman who was living an immoral life in the city, a prostitute, upon hearing that Jesus was a guest in Simon's house, came into the house uninvited with an alabaster vase of ointment. Crouching behind Jesus, at his feet, and weeping all the time, she anointed his feet with the ointment. His feet were wet with her tears, and she dried them with her hair.[2] When Jesus made no attempt to put a stop to this extraordinary and frankly erotic intrusion, Simon, true to his Pharisaic principles, said to himself, "If this man were a real prophet, he would know who this woman is who is touching him and what kind of woman she is." Since he *was* a real prophet, Jesus read Simon's thoughts. And so it was Simon's reaction that became the cue for the parable addressed to him by Jesus.

After Simon replied, no doubt wondering what was going on, Jesus spelled out for him the meaning of the parable, applying it to the situation created by the woman: "Then turning toward the woman he said to Simon, 'Do you see this woman? I entered your house, you gave me no water for my feet, but she has wet my feet with her tears and wiped them with her hair. You gave me no kiss, but from the time I came in she has not ceased to kiss my feet. You did not anoint my head with oil, but she has anointed my feet with ointment. Therefore I tell you, her sins, which are many, are forgiven, for she loved much; but he who is forgiven little, loves little.' And he said to her, 'Your sins are forgiven'" (Luke 7:44–48). Not all readers will agree with this rendering of Jesus's statement, but the principal point is that it must be consistent with the parable, according to which love follows forgiveness of debts. In fact, some commentators hold that Jesus's statement, "He who is forgiven little, loves little" (7:47), is editorial: added to confirm more completely the point of the parable. It seems that the woman had already encountered Jesus and received forgiveness, which Jesus now confirms in the presence of Simon and other scandalized guests before commending her faith in him as the way to God's forgiveness, then bidding her farewell. This is one beautiful story.

Similar Incidents in Other Gospels

The setting of the parable, but not the parable itself, is closely related to a similar incident in the other three Gospels. All three locate it in Bethany in the final phase of Jesus's life. Matthew (26:6–13) and Mark (14:3–9) identify the host as Simon the leper, while in the fourth Gospel (John 12:1–8), it takes place in the presence of Lazarus, raised from the dead by Jesus, while his sister Martha served and Mary, the other sister, anointed the feet of Jesus and dried them with her hair. In Matthew and Mark, the woman anoints the head, not the feet, of Jesus. As is the case throughout the Gospel, Luke has borrowed some elements from Mark, but the theme, dictated by the parable, gives the Lukan version a quite distinctive character.

We pray in the Lord's Prayer for the forgiveness that only God confers, and here Luke presents God as doing so by analogy with the forgiveness of debts. In following the example of the creditor in the parable, it is possible to confer on money matters a quality of compassion, generosity, and moral sensitivity often absent from financial transactions.

The Parable of the Good Samaritan (Luke 10:25–37)

The parable of the two debtors opens with a question that Jesus addresses to a Pharisee; this second parable is introduced by a question addressed to Jesus by a lawyer—a disingenuous question as it happens, since this specialist in *torah* wants to find out whether Jesus is, so to speak, orthodox. The question is, What must I do to inherit eternal life? Rather than answering it, Jesus responds with a question of his own (two questions, in fact): "What is written in the law? What is your reading of it?" In other words, tell me what *torah* has to say in answer to your question. The lawyer answers by citing a text from Deuteronomy: "You shall love the Lord your God with all your heart, and with all your soul, and with all your might" (6:5). He combines this with a text from Leviticus: "You shall love your neighbor as yourself: I am the Lord" (19:18). The answer is interesting for two reasons.

First, the citation is not from the Decalogue, as we might have expected from a lawyer, but from Deuteronomy 6:5, one of several statements in that book about the love of God expressed through observance of the law (Deut 10:12; 11:1; 13:22). In other words, the lawyer chooses quite correctly to take *torah* as referring not to specific laws but to the Pentateuch as a whole.

Second, Deuteronomy 6:5 is linked with Leviticus 19:18, the command to love your neighbor. Like Simon the Pharisee in the parable of the grateful debtors, the lawyer is commended for giving the correct answer, which, of course, is Luke's answer. However, in the similar questioning of Jesus in Matthew 22:34–40 and

Mark 12:28–34 about the greatest commandment in the law, Jesus replies by citing the same texts, but in this case, Deuteronomy 6:4–5 is the first and Leviticus 19:18 is the second in importance among the commandments. The authsor of the early Christian *Didache* (*The Teaching of the Twelve Apostles*) seems to have followed this alternative, since it begins as follows: "There are two ways, one of life and one of death, and there is a great difference between these two ways. This is the way of life: First, you shall love God who made you. Second, you shall love your neighbor as yourself."[3] By making them one law, Luke is implying that love of God and love of neighbor are inseparable. In other words, you cannot claim to love God if you do not love your neighbor. Your love of God is manifested in your love of your neighbor. This is to make the same point in a more formal way, which had already been stated in the Pauline correspondence: "The whole law is fulfilled in one word, 'You shall love your neighbor as yourself'" (Gal 5:14), or more succinctly, "Love is the fulfillment of the law" (Rom 13:9, my paraphrase). James, writing to the churches dispersed in lands outside Palestine, has the same message: "If you really fulfil the royal law, according to the scripture, 'You shall love your neighbor as yourself,' you do well" (Jas 2:8).

Who Is My Neighbor?

Feeling that he was losing control of the conversation, the expert in the law came up with a further question—"But who is my neighbor?"—which provided the occasion for the parable. It is true that the Hebrew term for neighbor (*rēʿa*), like the corresponding Greek term (*plēsíon*), can have several meanings, including someone in physical proximity, as, for example, a next-door neighbor, companion, or friend in addition to a fellow Hebrew, a fellow Israelite or Jew, or depending on the context, a fellow Christian. In the present context, however, and especially in a discussion about the law, it would be natural to assume that the term has an ethnic-religious connotation. There are numerous examples of this usage, including the last two laws of the Decalogue, but the term is also used with this reference in nonlegal contexts. For example, in Egypt, the day after assassinating an Egyptian who was beating a fellow Hebrew, the young Moses broke up a fight between two Hebrew men and reproached the one he took to be in the wrong, asking him, "Why are you beating up on your fellow-Hebrew [*rēʿa*]?" (Exod 2:13, my translation). There are occasions where the context leaves the reference ambiguous, and there is more than one way of referring to a fellow Hebrew or Israelite, and therefore there is some fluidity in usage. After the idolatrous calf worship in the wilderness, Moses instructed the Levites to go through the camp from gate to gate and kill their "brothers" (*ʾāḥîm*), "neighbors" (*rēʿîm*), and "those near to [them]" (*qĕrōbîm*; Exod 32:27, my translation). Since the only idolaters of concern to Moses were his fellow Hebrews, it seems that all three terms have this reference.

The Parable

To answer the lawyer's question about the scope of the term *neighbor*, Jesus tells a story that can be categorized as realistic fiction.

> A man on the well-travelled route from Jerusalem to Jericho was ambushed by robbers who stripped him, beat him up, robbed him of everything he had, and left him lying half-dead by the side of the road. The first person to pass that way was a priest who, thinking the man was dead, and afraid that he would be rendered unclean by contact with a corpse, crossed over to the other side and continued his journey. The same with a Levite belonging to the class next in importance in the temple hierarchy. Perhaps they were both on their way to the Jerusalem temple; we are not told. The third to pass that way was a Samaritan. Feeling sorry for this victim of violence and theft, he knelt beside him, there and then took what care he could of his wounds, bandaged them, sat him on his mule, and led him to the nearest inn where he stayed with him that night. The next day he handed over to the innkeeper the significant sum of two denarii, the equivalent

> of two days salary for agricultural workers, instructing him to treat the victim of the attack and look after him at his, the Samaritan's, own expense. He also promised to cover the innkeeper's expenses on his return journey back to Jerusalem. (Luke 10:29–37, my paraphrase)

The answer to Jesus's second question—Which of the three actors in this little drama was neighbor to the man ambushed by robbers?—is blindingly obvious. The lawyer agrees and is urged to imitate the Samaritan. Wealth is one means of relating to others, our neighbors, especially those in need, and we have seen that in Luke's Gospel, sin is in the first place relational, as is charity, or grace, or whatever term we use in describing a relation to others, which is the opposite and negation of sin. The Samaritan provides an excellent example of the positive use of money and other resources in caring for the neighbor in need.

The parable is another example of Luke's representation of the way Jesus taught by contrast. Think of the rich man and Lazarus or, in this instance, the juxtaposition of high-ranking temple clergy with the Samaritan, a member of a dissident, despised, and generally hostile group with their own place of worship and religious practices. A similar procedure is at work in the account of the healing of ten lepers, only one of whom, a Samaritan, therefore considered to all intents and purposes a foreigner (Greek: *allogenēs*), returned to thank Jesus (Luke 17:11–19). Samaritans and Jews simply avoided each other, as the woman with whom Jesus struck up a conversation at Jacob's well in John's Gospel reminded him "How is it that you, a Jew, ask a drink of me, a woman of Samaria?" (John 4:9). The Samaritans exploited their location between Galilee and Judaea to make life difficult for pilgrims and others traveling in either direction. On his way to Jerusalem, Jesus himself was refused hospitality in a Samaritan village (Luke 9:51–56). The historian Josephus tells us that Samaritans often waylaid and murdered Galileans who were on their way to worship in the Jerusalem temple (*Ant* 20:118; *BJ* 2:232–33), and he records elsewhere how on one occasion, Samaritans secretly entered the temple in Jerusalem and polluted it by scattering human bones in it during Passover (*Ant* 18:30). The contrast between priest and Levite on the one hand and a Samaritan on the other could hardly have been greater.

The Parable of the Rich Fool (Luke 12:13–21)

This parable is found only in Luke, though the apocryphal *Gospel of Thomas* (§63) has an abbreviated version with the same theme.[4] It is a theme that occurs rather frequently in classical literature—for example, in Seneca's *Epistulae Morales*. The occasion was a request from a man in the crowd for Jesus to persuade his brother to divide the family estate with him (Luke 12:13–15). Jesus declined the request on the not entirely serious grounds that he was not authorized to do so, but he took the occasion to address those present—including, no doubt, his disciples—on a related but more basic issue: "Take heed, and beware of all covetousness; for a man's life does not consist in the abundance of his possessions" (12:15).

Pleonexia, Greed

The Greek term corresponding to "greed" or "avarice" is *pleonexia*, usually with reference to an inordinate desire for more and more wealth, much more than is necessary for a satisfactory and productive life. For moralists and religious writers in the Greco-Roman period, who valued the virtue of moderation much more than is common in the contemporary world, *pleonexia*, or excess, was one of the worst vices. It features in the catalog of vices in Romans 1:28–29, and in the list in Colossians 3:5, it is even described as a form of idolatry. Jesus takes the occasion to issue a warning to those around him not against wealth in itself but against the inordinate desire for accumulating more and more wealth. He then told them a story to illustrate the warning.

The Parable

The parable reads as follows:

> The land of a rich man brought forth plentifully; and he thought to himself, "What shall I do, for I have nowhere to store my crops?" And he said, "I will do this: I will pull down my barns, and build larger ones; and there I will store all my grain and my goods. And I will say to my soul, Soul, you have ample goods laid up for many years; take your ease, eat, drink, be merry." But God said to him, "Fool! This night your soul is required of you; and the things you have prepared, whose will they be?" So is he who lays up treasure for himself, and is not rich toward God. (Luke 12:16–21)

This parable is unique in one respect: there is only one character, and he speaks only to himself. He is a wealthy man like the rich man who neglected Lazarus, except that he is a farmer, and we hear nothing about his expensive clothing, perhaps not considered appropriate for farmers. He reveals his concerns, ambitions, and what he thinks of life in general through his soliloquy. He is totally self-absorbed, he speaks only to himself, and we begin to imagine already how this will end in the final scene, no doubt often repeated throughout the centuries: a rich person surrounded by every amenity and comfort, living and dying alone without acquaintances or friends, talking to himself. His single-minded concentration on the accumulation of wealth has left no room for either God or fellow human beings. But God enters into the scene anyway in what is perhaps a unique intrusion in Luke's parables. Since the wealthy farmer is to die at night, the night following his self-congratulatory musings, the intervention may have come to him in a dream. In that context, the folly imputed to him implies not only stupidity but impiety.[5] The lesson is well summed up in the final statement, perhaps added by an early reader of the parable: "So is he who lays up treasure for himself, and is not rich toward God" (Luke 12:21).

Related Issues

The parable is followed by admonitions directed explicitly at the disciples and, by implication, at those early Christian communities with several of which Luke would have been familiar. The warning is against anxiety and solicitude, so often connected with money: anxiety of the kind that is literally soul-destroying, the kind that overwhelmed the man in the parable. The link between the parable and the admonitions that follow is the term *psyche*, meaning "the soul" or, to put it more analytically, "the seat and center of the inner life" (Luke 12:19–20, 22–23).[6] The emphasis now is on food and clothing, both dependent on money. The examples are taken from nature. Crows neither sow nor reap, they have no warehouses or barns, but they seem to do quite well on the whole, feeding on the goodness of a world created by God and not lacking in self-confidence. Wildflowers neither spin nor weave, they just exist, but not even Solomon's royal robes made by skilled human hands can match their beauty. One must, of course, do what is necessary in order to eat and be clothed, but the task imposed on the disciples of Jesus and the members of Christian communities is to do this without allowing these basic needs to consume all one's energy and obscure what is most important: the inner life, summed up here as seeking the kingdom of God proclaimed by Jesus.

The Parable of the Son Lost and Found

Like the previous two parables, this one is located in Luke's account of the journey narrative of Jesus from Galilee to Jerusalem, where he would fulfill his destiny (Luke 9:31–19:27). Jesus has many encounters in the course of this journey, with would-be disciples (9:57–62), lawyers (10:25), scribes (11:54), Pharisees, and in this instance, tax collectors and other unloved members of society (15:1–2) The parable of the son lost and found is introduced by two parallel pieces, also called parables: the finding of the lost sheep (15:3–7) and the finding of the lost coin (15:8–10). The first is about a man and the second about a woman, but both are about losing and then finding something of value. The assembly of this section, which coincides with the entire fifteenth chapter of the Gospel, clearly involved editorial activity, on the details of which the commentators are not in agreement.[7] It will suffice for the moment to say that the theme that binds the entire section together is the sadness of loss, loss of something or someone of great value, and the joy of finding that someone or something. Compare "This my son was dead, and is alive again; he was lost, and is found" (15:24) with the concluding verses to the two introductory narratives: "There will be more joy in heaven over one sinner who repents than over ninety-nine righteous persons who need no repentance" (15:7) and "There is joy before the angels of God over one sinner who repents" (15:10). As we read and take it in, we participate in the joy of God.

The Good Shepherd

I note in passing how frequent the theme of the Good Shepherd is both in early Christianity and in Christian art and hymns.[8] It should also be noted that in reading cautionary or moral stories of this kind, as with reading similar types of fiction, we are occasionally invited to suppress somewhat our critical faculties. We might be tempted to think, for example, that leaving ninety-nine sheep in the wilderness and going in search of the one stray might be a good way to lose a hundred sheep, but the author has neither the time nor the inclination to explain everything in detail: for example, that before setting out after the stray, he herded the ninety-nine into an open or enclosed sheepfold. Likewise with the woman who, every time she loses an expensive coin, rounds up the neighboring women and invites them to rejoice with her. (If we listen carefully, we will hear them saying sotto voce, "Oh no, not again!") In any case, these two little exempla are only there to introduce the story about the son lost and found.

The Parable as a Three-Act Drama

If this parable were to be made into a film or a play, it would probably be in three acts. It might be presented therefore as follows.

Act One

> There was once a man who had two sons. The younger of the two said to his father, "Father, give me the share of the property that belongs to me by right." So the father divided the property between them. A few days later, the younger son gathered together all he had, turned it into cash, and set off for a distant country, where he squandered all that he had in dissolute living. After he had spent everything, a severe famine fell on that country, and he was in great need. He went and took on a job with one of the citizens of that region, who sent him out into the farm to look after the pigs. He would gladly have filled his stomach with the pods that the pigs were eating, but no one gave him anything.

Act Two

> When he came to his senses, he thought, "How many of my father's hired hands have plenty to eat, and I am starving to death? I will go at once to my father, and I will say to him, 'Father, I have sinned against God and against you. I am no longer worthy to be called your son; treat me like one of your hired hands.'" So he set out for his father's house. While he was still a long way off, his father saw him and, moved to compassion, ran to meet him, threw his arms around him, and kissed him. His son said to him, "Father, I have sinned against God and against you; I am no longer worthy to be called your son." But the father said to his servants, "Quick, fetch a robe, the best we have, put it on him, and put a ring on his finger and sandals on his feet. Get the fatted calf, kill it, and let us celebrate with a feast. This son of mine was dead and has come back to life, was lost and now is found."

Act Three

His elder son had been out working on the farm, and on his way back, as he was approaching the house, heard the sound of music and dancing. He called one of the servants and asked him what it was all about. The servant replied, "Your brother has come, and your father has had the fatted calf killed because he has gotten him back safe and sound." His brother was angry and refused to go in, so his father went out and started to plead with him, but in reply, the brother said to his father, "For all these years I have been working like a slave for you and I never disobeyed your orders, but you have never once given me even a goat to have a slap-up meal with my friends. But no sooner does this son of yours show up, after going through all your property with prostitutes, than you kill the fatted calf for him." Then the father said to him, "Son, you are always with me, and everything that is mine is yours. How could we not celebrate and rejoice? Your brother was dead and has come back to life; he was lost and has been found." (my paraphrase)

The Parables of the Lost Sheep and the Lost Coin

The parable of the lost son, preceded by the miniparables of the lost sheep and the lost coin, was narrated in the presence of tax collectors and public sinners of one kind or another, and sure enough, also present were the Pharisees and scribes who, by this time, were following Jesus around to condemn him for associating with such people. There is what reads like an abbreviated version of the parable of the lost sheep in Matthew 18:10–14 and the *Gospel of Thomas* §107, but only the version in Luke communicates the relief and joy of the shepherd in finding this feckless animal that, like all sheep, is at a loss about what to do and how to avoid danger when separated from the flock. He wraps the sheep around his shoulders, carries it back home to safety, and calls his neighbors and friends to share his joy in finding it. Using the familiar figure of the sheep and the shepherd, the story ends by referring to God's joy in the repentant sinner, which is greater than God's joy in the ninety-nine who need no repentance.[9]

Inheriting in Custom and Law

These two preliminary episodes provide the preview for the story of the son lost and found and create the mood for listening to it. Something should, however, first be said about its social and economic substructure. Questions about the inheritance of family property have always been an important aspect of the domestic economy, but this was especially true of societies in the premodern period. In ancient Israel, inheritance played a crucial role in the economy of the clan (Hebrew: *mišpāhāh*), intermediate between the tribe (*šēbet*, *matteh*) and the individual domestic household (*bêt 'ab*, or "paternal household"). Much was at stake in passing on the property of the clan or the individual household to the next generation. In an agrarian society like that of ancient Israel, it would usually be a plot of land for farming, growing corn, and grazing herds, mostly sheep and goats. This was essential for the survival of the unit (e.g., Matt 10:6; 25:32–33; 26:31; John 10:1–16, 26–27; 21:15–16). At a deeper level, the clan or household was responsible not only to posterity but to the ancestors, who were considered as still belonging to the household and whose burial on its land was a sacred duty imposed on the family members. A classic case is that of Naboth of Jezreel. King Ahab of Samaria offered to buy his vineyard, which was close to the royal palace, or provide him with a better vineyard somewhere else. Naboth replied, "The Lord forbid that I should give you the inheritance of my fathers" and paid with his life for his answer (1 Kgs 21:1–4). Of several individuals, we hear that they were "gathered to the ancestors," which we may paraphrase as incorporation into the totality of the kinship unit. According to custom and law, sons received a portion of the property, and the firstborn son a double portion,[10] but this privilege of the firstborn could also be lost, as Reuben found out after committing incest (Gen 49:3–4). These decisions about the disposal of family property could be made by drawing up a will to go into effect after the father's death, or the will could be made and executed by the father during his lifetime. The beneficiaries would be male children, but according to the decision of Moses in the case of the five daughters of Zelophehad, whose father died without male offspring, a woman could inherit in the absence of a male heir (Num 27:1–11; 36:1–4; Josh 17:3–6). This did not prevent Rachel and Leah from complaining bitterly that they were ignored and regarded as outsiders in the distribution of family property (Gen 35:14–16). It seems that widows could also inherit the property of their deceased husbands, judging by the cases of the widow helped by the prophet Elisha (2 Kgs 8:1–6); Naomi, widow of Elimelech (Ruth 4:3); and Judith, widow of Manasseh (Jdt 8:7). Sale of the birthright of the firstborn son was forbidden, but this did not stop Esau from selling it to Jacob (Gen 25:31–34).

Lessons Taught by the Parable

At the level of everyday social and personal economics, one lesson is about the temptation presented by large amounts of money to satisfy instant gratification, ignoring other life values, including family, friends, and self-respect. As we proceed to act 2, the emphasis is on the possibility of repentance. The son first must repent to himself. Forgiveness demands that we confess our errors and, in the words of the Book of Common Prayer, "that we should not dissemble nor cloak them before the face of Almighty God our heavenly Father." The son makes the confession to himself (15:18), and he returns, no doubt with fear and misgivings, and repeats his confession in the presence of his father. (In ancient Hebrew, the verb "to return" is the same as "to repent.")[11] We note how the father receives him without hesitation, demands, or protocols. He goes out to meet him as he approaches; hugs and kisses him; fusses over him; provides him with a change of clothing, rings on his fingers, and new sandals; and ends with a celebratory feast. This image of God in relation to the repentant sinner is quite different from what some of us, as Christians of a certain age, have been accustomed to contemplating, for example, in some of the old prayers, hymns, and priestly admonitions.

9

TWO PARABLES ABOUT RICH MEN

The parables about the clever steward and the rich man and Lazarus make an impressive conclusion to Luke's storytelling and our study of the theme of wealth and poverty in Luke's Gospel. Before engaging with these last two parables in our list, we need to take account of the literary context in which both are placed, which is the sixteenth chapter of the Gospel. This chapter, which ends with the poor man in the bosom of Abraham and the rich man in Hades, begins with another parable, also exclusive to Luke, featuring a different kind of wealthy individual and a more direct approach to the use and abuse of wealth and possessions. Both parables begin with the same line—"There was a rich man"—indicating their function as bracketing a series of sayings that serve as commentary on both parables (16:9–18). There are six of these comments: three related to the story about the first rich man and his crafty estate agent (16:9–13) and the next three bearing on the story about the other rich man and the pauper Lazarus (16:16–18). In this apparently deliberate structure, the first set of three is separated from the second by a derogatory observation about Pharisees who had apparently heard the first of the two parables told by Jesus, perhaps even both, and had mocked Jesus, perhaps on account of what they took to be his naive understanding of financial matters, earning for them the reproach that they make a show of their righteousness in the public eye, but God sees through them and judges by different standards.

Chapter 16 therefore breaks down as follows:

The parable of the clever steward (16:1–8)
Three comments on this parable (16:9–13)
Pharisees mock and Jesus replies (16:14–15)
Three comments on the second parable (16:16–18)
The parable of the rich man and Lazarus (16:19–31)

In this apparently deliberate structure, the first set of three is separated from the second by a derogatory observation about Pharisees, as noted above. The problem then arises that this brief passage is out of context with the presentation of Pharisees in the Gospel, and in his second volume—the Acts of the Apostles—Pharisees are by no means hostile to the early disciples of Jesus, and we recall that Paul, with whom Luke seems to have been closely associated, was proud of his Pharisaic education.[1] However, before looking more closely at these comments, we must hear the parables that preceded them.

The Parable of the Clever Steward

Jesus said to his disciples:

> There was once a rich man who had a steward, and charges were brought against him that he had squandered his master's property. He summoned him and said to him, "What is this I hear about you? Give an account of your stewardship, for you can no longer be my steward." The steward said to himself, "What am I to do now that my master is dismissing me from my post? I'm not strong enough to dig, and I'm too ashamed to beg. I know what I will do so that, once dismissed from my post, there will be those who will welcome me into their homes." So, summoning his master's

> debtors one by one, he said to the first, "How much do you owe my master?" He replied, "A hundred jars of olive oil." The steward said to him, "Here, take your account, sit down, make it fifty, and be quick about it." To another he said, "And you, how much do you owe?" He replied, "A hundred measures of wheat." He said to him, "Here is your account; make it eighty." The master commended the dishonest steward for behaving so astutely, for in dealing with their own people, the children of this world are more astute than the children of light. (my translation)

This first of the two parables in chapter 16 features a steward or estate manager dismissed following accusations of mismanagement but who found a crafty way to soften the blow. The theme is the prudent use of money. Since he sees himself when dismissed by his wealthy employer, after a lifetime of estate management, as unfit for any other kind of job, he makes the rounds of the master's debtors in order to gain their goodwill by reducing their debts. This did not necessarily involve cheating his former employer, who, if this had been the case, would hardly have commended him for what he had done (16:8a). The allusion to "the dishonest steward" (16:8), the title the parable is generally given, would therefore refer to the original charge, which led to his termination—squandering his master's property, whatever that involved. What probably happened was that the steward forgave these tenants his commission as an estate agent, following the example of the creditor in another story of Jesus who forgave even larger debts (Luke 7:41–42).

Where precisely the parable ends is disputed. Assuming that it concludes with the commendation of the clever steward, with reference to the original cause for his dismissal, followed by the contrast between "the sons of this world" and "the sons of light" (Luke 16:8),[2] the three comments would begin with 16:9. They spell out the message, the point of the parable, for the benefit of the Christian hearers and readers, "the sons of light" for whom the Gospel was written. The three comments are linked by the key word *mammon*,[3] and all three deal with the use and abuse of wealth as indicated in the parable:

1. "I tell you, make friends for yourselves by means of unrighteous mammon, so that when it fails they may receive you into the eternal habitations" (Luke 16:9).

   This first comment makes a parallel between the astute behavior of the estate manager, one of the "sons of this world," and Jesus's recommendation to "the sons of light," those, in other words, who were his followers. The advice is to make friends by means of what worldly wealth you have so that, when it is gone, there may be those who will welcome you into "an eternal home."[4] It takes off from the musings of the estate manager about what he will do when unemployed and without shelter so that the tenants will welcome him into their homes (16:4). There may also be a muted anticipation of the parable of the rich man and Lazarus: if the rich man had used his worldly goods to bring relief to Lazarus and to others in the same wretched condition he would have been welcomed, perhaps by Lazarus himself, into the realm of the blessed, the eternal home. Or think of the tax collector Zacchaeus, short of stature but big of heart, who encountered Jesus on his triumphant entry into Jerusalem and promised to give away half his possessions to the poor and make amends to those whom he had cheated by repaying them fourfold. Jesus accepted him warmly, went home with him, and assured him that "today salvation has come to this house" (19:1–10). So according to this reading of the parable, the "friends" would be the poor, beneficiaries of the wealth of the rich, who would thus be the means for the salvation of the rich. As the French proverb has it, "La miséricorde de Dieu est infinie; elle sauvera même un riche" (God's mercy is infinite; it will even save a rich person).

2. "He who is faithful in a very little is faithful also in much; and he who is dishonest in a very little is dishonest also in much. If then you have not been faithful in the unrighteous mammon, who will entrust to you the true riches? And if you have not been faithful in that which is another's, who will give you that which is your own?" (16:10–12).

   This type of *a minore ad maiorem* argument applies the lesson of the parable to the Christian life, represented as a priceless gift from God, far greater than anything that wealth can bring, but a gift that demands perseverance, steadfast faith, and the proper uses of wealth, possessions, and resources alluded to in the fourfold repetition of the adjective *pistos* (trustworthy, faithful) and the verb *pisteuō* (believe, have complete confidence in something or someone).

3. "No servant can serve two masters; for either he will hate the one and love the other, or he will be devoted to the one and despise the other. You cannot serve God and mammon" (16:13).

   This third saying, which draws on the source shared by Matthew and Luke (known as Q, discussed earlier), encapsulates Luke's characteristically radical views on wealth and poverty set out in narrative form in the parable of the rich man and Lazarus and encountered frequently throughout the Gospel, often in the form of stark contrasts, opposites, and reversals. The phrasing is elegant in its simplicity: love-hate, devotion-contempt, God-money (*mammon*). On the one hand, the service is that of the "servants of the Lord," whose voice is heard often in Isaiah and Psalms; on the other hand, it is as if money is personified as a false idol called Mammon, which it is for many, as experience attests. To worship money is therefore to be in violation of the first commandment of the Decalogue, which is to worship God alone.

Since we take it that the next three comments bear on the second parable but precede it, a close reading of the last parable in our list must come first.

The Parable of the Rich Man and Lazarus (Luke 16:19–31)

> There was once a rich man who used to dress in purple and the finest linen and feasted sumptuously every day. At his gate lay a poor man named Lazarus, who was covered with sores. He would have been glad to satisfy his hunger with the scraps from the rich man's table. Dogs used to come and lick his sores. One day the poor man died and was carried away by the angels to be with Abraham. The rich man also died and was buried. In Hades, where he was in torment, he looked up, and there, far away, was Abraham with Lazarus close beside him. "Abraham, my father," he called out, "take pity on me! Send Lazarus to dip the tip of his finger in water, to cool my tongue, for I am in agony in this fire." But Abraham said, "Son, remember that the good things fell to you in your lifetime and the bad to Lazarus. Now he has his consolation here, and it is you who are in agony. But that is not all; there is a great gulf fixed between us; no one can cross it from our side to reach you, and none may pass from your side to us." "Then, father," he replied, "will you send him to my father's house, where I have five brothers, to warn them so that they may not come to this place of torment?" But Abraham said, "They have Moses and the prophets; let them listen to them." "No, father Abraham," he replied, "but if someone from the dead were to visit them, they would repent." Abraham answered, "If they do not listen to Moses and the prophets, they will pay no heed even if someone should rise from the dead." (my translation)

The Situation (16:19–21)

This parable is without parallel versions in the other Synoptic Gospels, and it is unique among Gospel parables in another respect: one of the principal characters has a name. Whether it was Luke's own composition or was handed down from Jesus himself by one or another of "those who from the beginning were eyewitnesses and ministers of the word" (Luke 1:2) or from those who put together "a narrative of the things which have been accomplished among us" (Luke 1:1), including the other Synoptic Gospel writers, or whether it was suggested by a moral fable in circulation in oral or written form in the surrounding culture has long been a subject of discussion. Whatever the source, Luke has made the parable his own, and it is consonant with what the third Gospel has to say elsewhere about the teaching of Jesus on wealth and poverty. Before undertaking our close reading, we should note a problem some commentators have experienced about the original unity of the parable. As Rudolph Bultmann pointed out long ago, the second brief conversation between the rich man and Abraham (Luke 16:27–31) deals with a different issue much debated in early Christian communities—namely, observance of the Old Testament law after the resurrection of Jesus.[5] We shall return to this issue, but first we must pose some questions about the dramatis personae of the story.

One question that comes to mind immediately is why the poor man is named and the rich man is not. In the absence of a name, the latter has been known since the Middle Ages—for example, in Chaucer and Langland—as Dives (in English, often one syllable), taken from the first line of the Vulgate version of the parable, *homo erat dives* (there was once a rich man).[6] Since this does not satisfy everyone, we learn from the commentators that over the years, attempts have been made to provide him with a name by recourse to similar stories from ancient Egypt, Greek-speaking lands, or a rabbinic text that tells of a wealthy tax collector called Ma'yan who died and had a splendid burial and a poor scholar who died unhonored. The fact remains that in the text as we have it, the rich man is anonymous.[7]

The description of the lifestyle of this conspicuously wealthy individual is succinctly conveyed by reference to clothing and food, important criteria then as now for identifying class and status. At that time, fine linen—especially in purple, the rarest of colors—connoted royalty or, at any rate, the high status and prestige that great wealth is thought by many to confer. As Jesus pointed out apropos of John the Baptist, soft garments and expensive apparel belong in the palaces of kings (Luke 7:25). Feasting sumptuously recalls an earlier parable, also unique to Luke, about a wealthy landowner and farmer who, after congratulating himself on having plenty of goods laid by for years to come, decides it is time to take life easy, eat, drink, and enjoy himself, and that same night, death takes him by surprise (12:19).

In a sense, the same two criteria—clothing and food—apply also to the poor man: his body is covered with sores rather than with fine purple linen, and he would have been content with scraps from the rich man's table rather than a sumptuous meal. The fact that he is given a name, a unique instance in Gospel parables, may be due to the author's wish to convey a stronger sense of actuality and to focus more directly on the often invisible poor. It may also have something to do with the choice of this particular name, as we shall see in due course. We may be surprised that he is given a Greek name, especially since the Semitic equivalent, Elazar (*'el'āzār*, meaning "God has helped me" or "May God help me," sometimes abbreviated to Lazar, *lā'zār*), is well attested in the Hebrew Bible and in ossuary inscriptions from the first centuries BCE and CE.[8] But Greek renderings of Hebrew-Aramaic names are also attested. Josephus, for example, mentions a certain Lazaros, father of Mannaios (*JW* 5:567), and a certain Eleazaros, a Jew of gigantic height—more than seven cubits tall—whom Herod the tetrarch gave as a gift to the emperor Tiberius (*Ant* 18:103).

About poor Lazarus, we are told that he was lying or squatting in front of the gate of the wealthy man. He may have been a former employee of this person, or someone may have deposited him there to beg for alms; we are not told. As with gated communities today, the gate served primarily to prevent uninvited humans and animals from encroaching on the property of the well-to-do. The rich man's gate provides another example of the parallels, links, antitheses, and reversals characteristic of Luke's Gospel in general and this parable in particular. *Here* the rich man is inside and the poor man is outside, looking in as the rich man dines sumptuously; *there*, after death, the poor man is inside banqueting with Abraham while the rich man is outside, looking in. To state the antithesis from a different angle, the poor man is outside the gate, while the rich man must pass through "the gates of Hades." There is even a dog, since we recall that the gates of Hades are guarded by the dreaded hound Cerberus, which permits no one to leave. The poor man is undernourished—starving, in fact, to the point where he would be glad to satisfy his hunger eating the scraps from the rich man's table. The same phrase, "longing to satisfy his hunger" (*epethumōn chortasthēnai*), is used in the parable of the lost son as we saw earlier, though in that case the food available to the younger son consists of the pods thrown to the pigs (Luke 15:16). Lazarus longing for the scraps from the rich man's table parallels the rich man in Hades longing to lick the water from Lazarus's fingertip.

The poor wretch is very ill, covered in ulcers, and dogs come and lick his sores. This last detail serves to emphasize more strongly his abject situation. Like the dogs assigned walk-on roles in a few biblical texts—for example, the dogs that feasted on the body of Jezebel—these are not sheepdogs, much less pets. They are wild dogs, the kind that live on what they can forage or the scraps thrown to them. The first tame dog we encounter in biblical and postbiblical texts is the unnamed canine that accompanied Tobias and the angel on their journey to Ecbatana (Tob 6:2; 11:4). In that respect, therefore, these dogs are, like Lazarus, eager to scavenge scraps: one more way in which the parallels and antitheses in the parable are interwoven.

Death and the Afterlife (16:22–23)

The turning point of the story, the *peripateia*, is the death first of the poor man, then of the rich man, and we are to assume that the latter followed soon after the former. Only the rich man can afford burial, presumably on a lavish scale proportionate to his wealth and lifestyle, and only the poor man is carried away by angels, thus rendering burial superfluous. The presence at the death of the righteous of angels who escort the dying person into the realm of the blessed is a familiar motif in ancient Judaic and Christian texts. It survives in the beautiful antiphon *In paradisum deducant te angeli* (May the angels escort you into paradise) in the Catholic Requiem Mass, which also mentions the angels who attended to Lazarus, who was at one time poor (*cum Lazaro quondam paupere*).

The destination of the rich man is different. Before proceeding, it is important to note that nowhere are we told that the rich man is wicked and the poor man righteous. The story is left to make its own point and carry its own meaning without authorial prompting. Also note that here, as elsewhere in Luke's Gospel, sin is in the first place relational. The most chilling feature of the story is that the rich man does not have to do anything in order to end up in Hades apart from continuing to live as he does *and to do so in the proximity of one sick and starving fellow human being*. It is assumed that the rich man was aware of this broken piece of humanity at his gate. In fact, it is clear from the appeal of the rich man in Hades to Abraham that he not only recognized the one-time pauper but even knew his name (Luke 16:24).

The poor man is led into the presence of Abraham, literally to Abraham's bosom (*eis ton kolpon abraam*). The image, unfamiliar to us today, is that of a meal at which the guests reclined rather than sitting on chairs, and the most favored guest occupied the place of honor, reclining in close proximity to the host. The poor man has therefore been invited as an honored guest to dine with Abraham; perhaps the author had in mind a kind of anticipation of the messianic banquet. It is worthy of note for future reference that apart from the present occasion, this figure of speech about the bosom occurs elsewhere in the New Testament only in the Gospel of John, and there only twice: God's only Son, who is in the bosom of the Father (John 1:18), and the disciple whom Jesus loved, who reclined "close to the breast of Jesus" at the Last Supper (13:23). We shall return later to this unnamed beloved disciple.

We come now to the postmortem situation of the conspicuously wealthy individual. Hades is short for the "House of Hades," and in Greek myth, Hades is king of the Underworld and Lord of the Dead, husband of Persephone and son of Chronos and Rea.[9] The Hades to which the rich man is assigned has, however, some features unique to this remarkable story. It differs from the Hades of Greek myth, which is the destination of all mortals. It also differs from the Hades of Revelation 20:13–14, according to which it is a kind of halfway house where the dead await the final judgment. The Greek translation of Psalm 16 in Acts 2:27, in which David (supposedly) predicts that God will not abandon Jesus in Hades (Hebrew: *Sheol*)—that is, to death and corruption—is also quite different. The destination of the rich man is closer to the fiery Gehenna, which frequently appears in the Gospels (e.g., Luke 12:5). Gehenna derives from the Hebrew *gē'-hinnom*, or "the valley of Hinnom," the valley south of the temple mound in Jerusalem (Wadi er-Rababeh). The site of idolatrous practices during the monarchy, at least from rabbinical times, it was the city dump, where rubbish was burnt. In prophetic texts, it is a place of punishment for the wicked. Isaiah 66:24, the last verse in the book, describes the elect gathering there to view the corpses of those who had rebelled against God. These corpses are consumed by worms and are burning in the fire: a scene of horror so bleak that the second-to-last verse was repeated after this verse in the synagogue liturgy (the *haftarah*) so as not to end the reading on such a distressing note.

Here, too, however, the parable has its unique features. From the Hades to which the rich man is consigned, you can see the realm of the blessed and even communicate orally over the abyss that separates the two locations. It is also possible to carry on a conversation while engulfed in flames. The one thing you cannot do is leave.

A First Exchange between the Rich Man and Abraham (16:24–26)

The rich man, in death still a son of Abraham, asks the great patriarch to grant him, through the agency of the poor man, the absolute minimum to reduce the torments of thirst (a fingertip dipped in water), as earlier the poor man sought the absolute minimum to reduce the pangs of hunger (scraps from the rich man's table). Abraham's response is chilling in its finality: "Son, remember that you in your lifetime received your good things, and Lazarus in like manner evil things; but now he is comforted here, and you are in anguish" (Luke 16:25). This may be the first time this conspicuously wealthy individual discovers that wealth does not necessarily give power to his words. Abraham then explains why it is impossible for Lazarus, now in the realm of the blessed, to visit Hades, the fiery abode of the dead: he informs the wealthy and anonymous man that between him in Hades and Lazarus in the realm of the blessed is a great gulf (*chasma mega*)—parallel to the *chasma* between the rich man at his table and the poor man outside the gate during their lifetimes.

At this juncture, the main point about the reversal in the condition of the two has been made. The parable could end here, and for those who read the rest of the narrative as originally a distinct composition with a different theme, it might well do so. But then we are left with the problem that Abraham's explanation of the situation (Luke 16:25) reads like a simple reversal of fortune, a statement of fact free of moral considerations: a lifetime of poverty, illness, and misery earns you a blessed postmortem existence; a lifetime of great wealth and pleasure, eating, drinking, and enjoying yourself, earns you a hereafter of misery and torment. You can have "good things" (*ta agatha*, 16:25) either during your lifetime or after death, but not both. Even though the rich man enjoyed these "good things" while ignoring the plight of Lazarus, we would expect some qualification of a moral nature to be added. The need for further clarification may, in fact, explain the second request of the rich man and the final reply of Abraham, which does introduce an explicit moral dimension—namely, consideration of the law of Moses and the teaching of the prophets. It even strengthens the case for the unity of the parable in spite of the different theme addressed in this final section. We should therefore consider the second request of the rich man before addressing this dilemma.

A Second Request Is Denied (16:27–31)

So we move on to the final phase. The rich man petitions that Lazarus be permitted to return from the dead on a different mission. He is to go to the five brothers of the rich man to warn them about their way of living, no doubt similar to his own and therefore leading to the same fate. This visitation fits the plot of the ghost story, both ancient and modern, in which the revenant appears to an individual to warn of the consequences of transgressive or criminal behavior. Abraham does not deny the possibility of this second visitation, but he replies bluntly that even the visit of one raised from the dead would be unavailing for those inattentive to the law of Moses and the teaching of the prophets.

Since the parable is a fictional genre, we might want to ask, before considering more closely the request and the reply, why the rich man makes his appeal for *five* brothers, since one would have made the point. It may be that five was considered a special, almost sacred number as the sum of the first two prime numbers, a fact well known to ancient mathematicians. The pentagram was held in great reverence by the disciples of Pythagoras, and five and multiples of five are of frequent occurrence in the Synoptic Gospels.[10] An alternative explanation may, however, be proposed. Given the impressive parallels and links between the third and the fourth Gospel noted by New Testament scholars, the interest in Luke's Gospel and the Gospel of John in the Samaritans, and especially the name

Lazarus, found only in the Gospels of Luke and John, we might consider the five previous "husbands" of the Samaritan woman with whom Jesus struck up a conversation by the well of Jacob, all presumably in need of a warning (John 4:7–26). This is speculative, of course, but it may explain the reference to the Law and the Prophets followed by the prohibition of adultery *with reference to men only* immediately preceding the parable, the intent of which *at that point* has long been in dispute (Luke 16:16–18).

Since Luke's Gospel was intended in the first place for Christians, and especially newly initiated Christians like the Theophilus to whom it is dedicated, this final word of Abraham about the necessity of observing the law and the prophets "even if someone should be raised from the dead" would inevitably have been read as referring to one of the most important and disputed issues among early Christian communities of the first two or three generations—namely, the continued relevance of the Mosaic law after the resurrection of Jesus. This was of primary importance for the Jerusalem circle under the leadership first of Peter and later of James, brother of Jesus, and also for Samaritan Christians and, later, the Christian sect known as Ebionites ("the poor"). It is also an important issue in the Pauline letters, but one that lies beyond the scope of our inquiry. Meanwhile, the possibility of someone being raised from the dead (Luke 16:31) obliges us to return once more to the poor man's name.

Lazarus of the Parable and Lazarus of Bethany

In the New Testament, only one person apart from the poor man in the parable bears the name Lazarus: the brother of Mary and Martha who, according to John 11:1–44, was raised from the dead by Jesus in Bethany. The Lazarus of Bethany and the Lazarus of the parable are both ill and both die; the former is raised from the dead, while the resurrection of Luke's Lazarus, already transported to the realm of the blessed by angels, is requested and denied. The point in both instances is to awaken faith. Abraham rejects the request from the rich man in Hades on the grounds that if the brothers pay no heed to Moses and the prophets, they would not believe even if someone were to come to them raised from the dead (Luke 16:31). With the other Lazarus, it is repeatedly and explicitly stated that Jesus raised him from the dead in order to awaken belief in himself and his mission (John 11:15, 25–27, 40, 42), and in fact, many who were not already attached to Jesus and who witnessed the event did believe in him (11:45; 12:11, 17–19). If the author of the parable had this account of a resurrection in mind, perhaps in an earlier version or circulating orally, it would have made the request of the rich man on behalf of his brothers appear more plausible.[11]

Some commentators have moved beyond this point by suggesting that the Lazarus of John's Gospel is the unnamed beloved disciple of Jesus who reclined on Jesus's bosom at the Last Supper (John 13:23), comparable therefore to the Lazarus who reclined on Abraham's bosom in the paradise of the blessed. We noted earlier that the only other biblical occurrence of this metaphor occurs in the Gospel of John, but with reference to Jesus, only Son of God, in the bosom of the Father (1:28). The love of Jesus for Lazarus of Bethany is noted in the account of his raising from the dead (11:3, 36). Then, soon afterward, we begin to hear about a beloved disciple who reclined "close to the breast of Jesus" at the Last Supper (13:21–26); was on familiar terms with the high priest during the trial of Jesus (18:15–16); was the only disciple present with Mary, the mother of Jesus, as Jesus died on the cross (19:25–27); outran Simon Peter to the tomb (20:2–9); and was the first to recognize Jesus after the resurrection by the Sea of Tiberias (21:7).

The commentators have, therefore, found it difficult to resist taking this further step of identifying Lazarus of Bethany and the beloved disciple as one and the same person.[12] As always, however, caution is in order. The disciple who reclined next to Jesus at the Last Supper (John 13:23–25) is referred to as the disciple "whom Jesus loved," which, in the form of "the beloved disciple," sounds like a fixed title or designation in common use in early Christian circles. Then again, Jesus loved Lazarus, but he also loved his sisters,

Martha and Mary (11:5). The mourners at the tomb of Lazarus in Bethany commented on the love of Jesus for Lazarus when they saw him weeping, but Jesus wept only when he saw Mary weeping, the same Mary—according to the author—who anointed Jesus's feet and dried them with her hair (11:1–2). So the identification of Lazarus raised from the dead with the beloved disciple is by no means obvious.[13]

A more formidable complication arises for those who identify the beloved disciple with John, brother of James and son of Zebedee, since this obviously rules out identification with Lazarus of Bethany. The cryptic statement toward the end of the fourth Gospel refuting the rumor that the beloved disciple would not die (John 21:20–23) is followed by a sentence that serves as the finale of the Gospel: "This is the disciple who is bearing witness to these things, and who has written these things; and we know that his testimony is true" (21:24). In effect, it identifies the same disciple as the author of the Gospel. It seems unlikely that John, the Galilean fisherman, authored the Gospel according to John.

As to how this link between the historical Lazarus of Bethany, brother of Martha and Mary and beloved by Jesus, and the fictional Lazarus of Luke's parable could have come about, we can only speculate. The name of the poor man in the parable whose resurrection was denied may have been suggested by a tradition, in either oral or written form, behind the account of the raising of Lazarus in John 11. Or perhaps the tradition about the name of the resurrected Lazarus was suggested by the Lukan story of Lazarus on the hypothesis that the parable, whether independently or in Luke's Gospel, was in circulation at the time of the composition of the fourth Gospel. This hypothesis may claim some support from the absence of the name Lazarus in the fourth Gospel previous to the miracle reported in the eleventh chapter. But in the present state of our knowledge, or rather ignorance, the matter cannot be decided beyond a reasonable doubt.

Three Comments on the Second Parable (Luke 16:16–18)

After the three comments on the first of the two parables and the repudiation of the Pharisees in attendance (16:9–15), there is a second series of three comments related more directly to the second parable, the rich man and Lazarus (16:16–18):

1. The law and the prophets were in effect until John (the Baptist); since then, the good news of the kingdom of God is proclaimed, and everyone tries to enter it by force.
2. It is easier for heaven and earth to come to an end than for one letter of the law to lose its force.
3. A man who divorces his wife and marries another commits adultery; and anyone who marries a woman divorced from her husband commits adultery.

These statements, with parallels in the Gospel according to Matthew, are presented as distinct sayings but are connected with the issue about the place of Mosaic law in the life of a Christian community. We encountered them at an earlier stage, but a few remarks may be added. With respect to the first and second, the point is that despite the distinction between the two epochs—the epoch of the law and the prophets ending with the John the Baptist's preaching and the epoch of the proclamation of the kingdom of God in the public activity of Jesus (Luke 1:1–2; Acts 1:1–2)—the law of Moses still retains its moral authority and force. Recall Abraham's reply to the rich man in Hades, that his five brothers need to pay attention to the law and the prophets, and his insistence that "if they do not hear Moses and the prophets, neither will they be convinced if some one should rise from the dead" (Luke 16:27–31). For the Christian to whom the parable is addressed, this would make an important point about the moral obligations of Christians after the resurrection of Jesus.

The categorical statement about the permanent relevance of the law is followed by a reiteration of the commandment of the Decalogue about adultery, but worded to apply to men only (cf. Exod 20:14; Deut 5:18). This third statement, which has nothing directly to do with wealth and poverty, has raised questions among commentators about its place and function at this point in the Gospel. It is presented as a saying of Jesus, but as more than one exegete has confessed, its raison d'être in this context is obscure. Why is the law forbidding adultery repeated at this point? How can it be a comment on the parable of the rich man and Lazarus? Why does it apply only to men? Bearing in mind that this is one of the comments on the second parable in this final series, the parable of the rich man and Lazarus, recall the second request of the rich man in Hades in favor of his five brothers and the proposal made earlier about a connection with the five former partners of the Samaritan woman with whom Jesus struck up a conversation at the well of Jacob in the fourth Gospel (John 4:18). These five may well have needed a reminder of the law about adultery worded with special reference to males. The proposal is speculative, but by this point, the message of the parable is clear.

10

SUMMARY

In the prologue to Acts, Luke describes his first volume as a record of what Jesus did and taught. What he did consisted in great measure of acts of healing, including healing by miraculous means, for the benefit of the most disadvantaged of society: first, the poor, but also the sick and disabled and, in general, those of low status least able to help themselves. This telling of the Jesus story has given equal attention to what he taught, either formally in the Sermon on the Plain or at different points of the story in conversation with disciples and encounters with individuals, groups, and the crowds of people who followed him wherever he went. Jesus's teachings touched on many aspects of human life, but there is a notable emphasis on the effect on the individual and society in general—either benign or corrupting—of wealth and possessions and their often grossly uneven distribution.

A dominant theme in Luke's account of the teaching of Jesus, including the six narrative parables unique to Luke's Gospel, is that it addresses different aspects of the use and misuse of wealth: the forgiveness of debt, concern for the poor and those who cannot help themselves, the futility of dedicating one's life to accumulating wealth and possessions, and the corrupting influence on society of gross inequality of wealth and a great gap between the rich and the poor. These themes are presented in vivid and lively colors in the six parables selected for closer consideration. With the exception of the first, they are located in the second major section of the Gospel, after Jesus decided to leave Galilee and go to Jerusalem (Luke 9:51) to face a trial and death, which he knew awaited him and which he had foretold more than once. We are constantly reminded in this second section that Jesus and the men and women who had thrown in their lot with him are on a journey. The mood becomes more ominous, the predictions more dire, as we approach the tremendous climax of the story of Jesus.

SUGGESTIONS FOR FURTHER READING

No attempt is made to provide a full bibliography. The following titles represent only a sample of commentaries and critical readings on Luke's Gospel and the theme of wealth and poverty, the rich and the poor, in that Gospel. Most are fairly recent, and all are in English—some translated from foreign languages, especially German.

Commentaries and Studies

Barrett, C. K. *Luke the Historian in Recent Study*. Philadelphia: Fortress, 1970.

Bultmann, Rudolph. *The History of the Synoptic Tradition*. Translated by J. Marsh. Rev. ed. New York: Harper & Row, 1976.

Conzelmann, Hans. *The Theology of Saint Luke*. Translated by G. Buswell. Philadelphia: Fortress, 1982.

Donahue, R., SJ. *The Gospel in Parable*. Philadelphia: Fortress, 1988.

Dunn, James D. G. *The Evidence for Jesus*. London: SCM, 1985.

———. *Who Was Jesus?* London: SPCK, 2016.

Fitzmyer, J. A. *The Gospel according to Luke I–IX*. Anchor Bible. New York: Doubleday, 1981.

———. *The Gospel according to Luke X–XXIV*. Anchor Bible. New York: Doubleday, 1985.

Flender, Helmut. *Saint Luke: Theologian of Redemptive History*. Translated by H. Reginald and I. Fuller. Philadelphia: Fortress, 1967.

Funk, R. W. *Parables and Presence*. Philadelphia: Fortress, 1982.

Jeremiah, Joachim. *The Parables of Jesus*. 3rd rev. ed. London: SCM, 1972.

Keck, L., and J. L. Martin, eds. *Studies in Luke–Acts*. New York: Abingdon, 1966.

Marshall, I. H. "Recent Study of the Gospel according to Luke." *Expository Times* 80 (October 1, 1968): 4–8.

Reicke, B. *The Gospel of Luke*. Translated by Ross Mackenzie. London: SPCK, 1965.

Wealth and Poverty, Rich and Poor in Luke's Gospel

Brown, Peter. *Treasure in Heaven: The Holy Poor in Early Christianity*. Charlottesville: University of Virginia Press, 2016.

Brueggemann, Walter. *Money and Possessions*. Louisville: Westminster / John Knox, 2016.

Cassidy, R. J. *Jesus, Politics, and Society: A Study of Luke's Gospel:* Maryknoll, NY: Orbis, 1978.

Coggins, Richard J. "The Old Testament and the Poor." *Expository Times* 99 (October 1987): 11–14.

Collins, John J. "Essenes." In *ABD*, edited by David Noel Freedman, 2:619–626. New York: Doubleday, 1992.

Domeris, W. R. "Biblical Perspectives on the Poor." *JTS* 57 (December 1986): 57–61.

Donahue, John R. "Two Decades of Research on the Rich and Poor in Luke-Acts." In *Justice and the Holy: Essays in Honor of Walter Harrelson*, edited by D. A. Knight and P. J. Paris, 129–144. Atlanta: Scholars Press, 1989.

Fitzmyer, Joseph A. "The Disciple's Right Use of Material Possessions." In *The Gospel according to Luke I–IX*, 247–251. AB 28. Garden City, NY: Doubleday, 1981.

Gillman, J. *Possessions and the Life of Faith: A Reading of Luke–Acts*. Collegeville, MN: Glazier, 1991.

Grant, F. C. *The Economic Background of the Gospels*. Oxford: Oxford University Press, 1926.

Hauerwas, Stanley. "The Politics of Charity." *Interpretation* 31 (1977): 251–262.

Johnson, Luke T. *The Literary Function of Possessions in Luke–Acts*. Missoula, MT: Scholars Press, 1977.

———. *Sharing Possessions: Mandate and Symbol of Faith*. OBT 9. Philadelphia: Fortress, 1981.

Nickelsburg, G. W. E. "Riches, the Rich, and God's Judgement in 1 Enoch 95–105 and the Gospel according to Luke." *NTS* 25 (1978–1979): 324–344.

O'Toole, R. T. "Poverty and Wealth in Luke-Acts." *Chicago Studies* 16 (1991): 29–41.

Roth, St. John. *The Blind, the Lame, and the Poor: Character Types in Luke–Acts*. Sheffield: Sheffield Academic Press, 1997.

NOTES

Chapter 1

1 The description of the taking up into heaven of Jesus is modeled on the taking up (ascension) of the prophet Elijah.

2 To the best of my knowledge, Luke has not been acknowledged as the patron saint of physicians, but he is regarded as the patron saint of painters. For Catholics and Orthodox Christians, he is a saint whose feast day is celebrated on October 18.

3 The title "John the Baptist" is unfortunately ambiguous, but there appears to be no acceptable alternative—not "the Baptizer" and certainly not "the Immerser."

Chapter 2

1 Elizabeth, married to the priest Zechariah, is *sungenis* with Mary—that is, belonging to the same extended family (Luke 1:7, 18). Though "well on in years," she was to have a son. Elizabeth and Mary were close enough for Mary to feel obliged to make the three-day journey from Galilee to be with her relative for the remaining five months of her pregnancy.

2 The name Jesus is the Greek equivalent of Joshua (Hebrew: *yehoshua*). Several other individuals bear the name Joshua in the Old and New Testaments.

3 The ambiguity lies in the phrase "after me" (Greek: *opiso mou*). Compare the statement of Jesus later in the Gospel: "If any man would

come after me [*opiso mou*], let him deny himself and take up his cross daily and follow me" (Luke 9:23).

4 The Hebrew term *sora'at*, often translated "leprosy" (Hansen's disease), includes other disfiguring diseases.

5 The reply of Jesus to the complaint of his mother, "Son, why have you treated us like this?" is somewhat obscure, but given the situation, the most likely translation is "Did you not know that I had to be in my Father's house?" For a thorough discussion of the options, see Joseph A. Fitzmyer, *The Gospel according to Luke I–IX*, AB 28A (Garden City, NY: Doubleday, 1981), 443–44.

Chapter 3

1 According to Hegesippus (in Eusebius, *Historia Ecclesiastica* 3.11; 32.1–4), Klopas was the brother of Joseph, father of Jesus.

2 Ancient Hebrew has five terms for "poor"—*dal*, *ebyon*, *'ani*, *'anaw*, and *rash*—the respective nuances of which are not always easy to detect. To make the point, the New Revised Standard Version (NRSV) translates *anaw* in Psalms with six different epithets: poor (Ps 22:27), meek (Pss 10:17; 37:11), afflicted (Ps 9:13), oppressed (Pss 10:12; 69:33), humble (Pss 25:9; 34:3), and downtrodden (Ps 147:6).

3 On Hanina, see G. Vermes, "Hanina ben Dosa: A Controversial Galilean Saint from the First Century of the Christian Era," *JJS* 23 (1972): 28–50; 24 (1973), 51–64; and J. Blenkinsopp, "Miracles: Elisha and Hanina ben Dosa," in *Miracles in Judaic and Christian Antiquity*, ed. J. C. Cavadini (Notre Dame, IN: University of Notre Dame Press, 1999), 57–82. On Honi, see A. Buchler, *Types of Judaic Palestinian Piety from 70 B.C.E. to 70 C.E.* (New York: KTAV, 1968), 196–264.

4 For the texts, see A. Cowley, *Aramaic Papyri of the Fifth Century B.C.* (Osnabrück, Germany: Otto Zeller, 1967), 44–50, 54–56.

Chapter 4

1 The baptism of John differed in several respects from the cultic lustrations of the Qumran community, as Hartmut Stegemann pointed out in *Die Essener, Qumran, Johannes der Täufer und Jesus. Ein Sachbuch* (Freiburg, Germany: Herder, 1993), but he failed to add that the

Qumran practice is called "The Waters of Repentance" (1QS III.9). Repentance was the essence of John's preaching.

2 On the Essenes, see J. J. Collins, "Essenes," in *ABD*, ed. David Noel Freedman (New York: Doubleday, 1992), 2:619:26; E. Schürer, *The History of the Judaic People in the Age of Jesus Christ*, ed. Geza Vermes, Emil Schürer, and Fergus Millar (Edinburgh: T&T Clark, 1979), 2:555–74, 583–90.

3 The citation from Isaiah 40:3–5, originally with reference to the repatriation of exiled Judeans from Babylon, is applied to the call for individual repentance, a change of life, addressed to John's hearers. Luke is here citing from the Greek (Septuagint) Version. The Hebrew reads (translated), "A voice cries: in the wilderness prepare the way for the Lord."

4 Hebrew *lehem*, "bread," can also stand for food in general.

Chapter 5

1 Thomas Hobbes, "Of Miracles and Their Use," in *Leviathan*, ed. C. B. Macpherson (Harmondsworth, UK: Penguin, 1968), chap. 37.

2 See the survey of opinions on miracles in Randall C. Zachman, "The Meaning of Biblical Miracles," in Cavadini, *Miracles in Judaic and Christian Antiquity*, 1–18.

3 Assuming this to be true, this would be the synagogue on the site of which the present Capernaum synagogue, familiar to pilgrims and tourists, is located.

4 The word used in the Matthean version is *pais* (child), but the same term occurs in the Lukan version together with *doulos* (slave or servant), which suggests that *pais* could also refer to a servant.

5 For some of the more benign miracles of Elisha, see J. Blenkinsopp, "Miracles: Elisha and Hanina ben Dosa," in Cavadini, *Miracles in Judaic and Christian Antiquity*, 57–81.

6 The raising to life of Lazarus, reported only in the fourth Gospel (John 11:1–44) is unique in that Lazarus was a friend close to Jesus and the miracle came about at the implied request of the sisters of Lazarus, Mary and Martha, also close friends of Jesus. It is unique in another respect, in that Lazarus had been dead four days and corruption had already set in when Jesus intervened (John 11:17, 39).

7 That Jesus said "wake up" instead of "arise" or "get up" is consistent with his previous statement that she was not dead but sleeping. This

meaning of the Greek verb *egeiro* is well attested in this sense (e.g., Matt 1:24; 8:25; 25:7; Mark 4:38; Acts 12:7; Rom 13:11).

Chapter 6

1 What Mary said to Gabriel, literally translated, is "I do not know a man." In Hebrew, the verb "to know" (*yāda*) is used in the Hebrew Bible and elsewhere for sexual relations, beginning with Adam and Eve (Gen 4:1).

2 Confusion about the date of the census is also in evidence in Acts 5:36–37, where Gamaliel, teacher of the law, states that Judah the Galilean revolted at the time of the census and that his revolt followed that of Theudas. According to Josephus, however, the revolt of Theudas took place under the procurator Cuspius Fadus, Roman-appointed governor in 44–45 BCE (*Ant* 20:5.1).

3 Jesus is often referred to as "Jesus of Nazareth" (Luke 4:34; 18:37; 24:19).

4 It is worth noting that in Jesus's time, twelve years of age signified the passage from childhood to maturity, bringing with it a degree of responsibility to observe the stipulations of the law (m. Niddah 5:6). Josephus notes that Samuel initiated his prophetic career after completing his twelfth year (*Ant* 5 par. 348).

5 On the second-century BCE apocryphal gospels, such as *The Gospel of Pseudo-Matthew*, *The Gospel of Thomas*, and similar works, see M. R. James, *The Apocryphal New Testament* (Oxford: Clarendon, 1983) (original edition 1924), 38–90. Montague Rhodes James was also famous as an author of ghost stories. Among the numerous reconstructions of the "lost years" down to the present, I mention only one, the *Vie de Jésus* of Ernest Renan, which is less wild than its early predecessors but much more sentimentalized than the apocryphal works.

6 Johanan ben Zakkai: "Galilee, Galilee, you hate the Torah, your end will be destruction" (y. Shabb. 16:8).

7 Enclosure and seizure of peasant holdings was from ancient times a problem in Palestine, as Isaiah attests in pronouncing a woe on "those who join house to house, who add field to field, until there is no more room" (Isa 5:8).

8 The name means "the village" (Hebrew: *kefar*) of Nahum, perhaps in reference to the prophet of that name.

9 Attestations from Josephus, *Judaic War* 3:509, 520; and Strabo, *Geographica* 16:2.45. The Gospels also attest to the prominence of fish in the Palestinian diet at that time: the feeding of the five thousand with bread and fish (Luke 9:12–17), the child who asks for a fish and is given a snake (11:11), the risen Jesus who is offered broiled fish by his followers in Jerusalem (24:42), and fish for breakfast by the Sea of Galilee (John 21:9–12).

10 Sean Freyne, *Jesus, a Jewish Galilean: A New Reading of the Jesus-Story* (London: T&T Clark International, 2004), 24–59.

11 Luke has them going through the *keramoi*, the tiles made of baked brick, in keeping with what would have been familiar to his hellenistic readers. Getting a sick man on a pallet through a typical Palestinian roof made of wooden beams overlaid with clay and rushes would have been a challenge, but not one beyond the capacity of two or more robust bearers.

Chapter 7

1 The Gospel ends, after Jesus finally departs from his disciples, with his disciples praising God together in the temple (Luke 24:53). Acts begins with the first Christian cell in Jerusalem spending much time together in prayer in the temple and celebrating the eucharistic meal together in their homes (Acts 2:42). On frequentation of the temple, see also Acts 3:1, 3; 4:1; 5:20–21; 21:27–28; 22:17; 26:21.

2 The alternative textual reading of Luke 10:1 and 10:17 is "seventy" for "seventy-two," resting on an alternative counting of the descendants of Noah's sons: Shem, Ham, and Japhet (Gen 10).

3 Note that English translations sometimes use words other than "poor" for the Hebrew *anawim*—for example, "humble" or "oppressed."

4 Alternatively and more incisively in the Revised English Bible, "There must be no limit to your goodness, as your heavenly Father's goodness knows no bounds" (Matt 5:48).

5 These formulations are based on the English translation of Walter Bauer's *Griechisch-Deutsches Wörterbuch*: *A Greek-English Lexicon of the New Testament and Other Early Christian Literature*, 3rd rev. ed., ed. F. W. Danker (Chicago: University of Chicago Press, 2000), 677–78.

6 Jesus continued to teach in the postresurrection period, including to the two disciples on the way to Emmaus (Luke 24:25–27) and to the Eleven in Jerusalem (24:45–49).

7 Cf. Matt 5:31–32. Luke omits the phrase about divorce "except on the ground of unchastity" in the Matthean version.
8 With respect to Zechariah and Elizabeth (Luke 1:5–6), the ritual post-partum purification of Mary (2:22–24), the presentation of Jesus in the temple according to the law (2:27), and Jesus's parents, who fulfilled all requirements of the law (2:39).
9 The same text is cited toward the beginning of Luke's Gospel (3:4–6).

Chapter 8

1 The denarius was a silver coin that for centuries was standard currency throughout the Roman Empire. It is generally taken to correspond to the salary of one working day for an agricultural laborer, as in the parable on the laborers in the vineyard (Matt 20:1–2).
2 Since this was a special meal, Simon and his guests would have reclined rather than being seated side by side. Hence Jesus's feet, from which his sandals would have been removed on arrival, would therefore have been behind rather than under the table.
3 *Didache* or *The Teaching of the Twelve Apostles* 1:2. On this early Christian text, see M. W. Holmes, ed., *The Apostolic Fathers* (Grand Rapids, MI: Baker Academic, 1992), 334–69.
4 Jesus said, "There was a rich person who had a great deal of money. He said: 'I shall invest my money so that I may sow, reap, plant, and fill my storehouses with produce, so that I may lack nothing.' These were the things he was thinking in his mind, but that very night he died. Whoever has ears should hear." Martin Meyer, trans., *The Gospel of Thomas: The Hidden Sayings of Jesus* (San Francisco: Harper, 1992), 47.
5 In ancient Hebrew, *nabal* (fool) often implies impiety in addition to folly—for example, in Psalms 14:1 and 53:1, where the *nabal* proclaims, "There is no God."
6 I take this definition from Danker, *Greek-English Lexicon*, 1099.
7 For details and bibliography, see J. A. Fitzmyer, *The Gospel according to Luke X–XXIV*, AB 28A (Garden City, NY: Doubleday, 1985) 1071–94.
8 Matt 18:12–14; *The Gospel according to Thomas* #107; *The Apocryphal Gospel of Truth* 31:35–32:9; Jesus as the good shepherd in John 10:11–18.
9 The history of the iconography of the good shepherd would call for its own study. This is a task for the specialist in art history and the history

of music or for a biblical scholar whose primary interest is in reception history. I may, however, mention one early example: the statuette of Jesus as the good shepherd with a lamb or sheep on his shoulders, just like the shepherd in the parable (Luke 15:5). It is now in the Museo Cristiano Pio Lateranense in Rome but originally came from one of the catacombs.

10 Deut 2:15–17. To the firstborn is allotted *pî šenayîm*, "two-thirds," but in this context, it is a double portion.

11 The Hebrew substantive *tĕšûbah* and the corresponding verb *šûb* are used with reference to both returning and repenting.

Chapter 9

1 Acts 23:6–10; 26:5. In his self-presentation to the Romans (Rom 1:1), Paul's description of himself as *aphorismenos* (set apart) reproduces the consonants of Hebrew *pĕrûšî* (Pharisee), perhaps not by accident.

2 The expression "children of light" occurs frequently in the Qumran texts (e.g., 1QS 1:9; 2:16) and occasionally in the New Testament (John 12:36; 1 Thess 5:5; Eph 5:8). It probably originated in a sectarian context.

3 This term, of uncertain derivation, is not attested in the Hebrew Bible and is rare in the New Testament, but it occurs occasionally in the Targums and rabbinic texts—for example, m. Aboth 2:17, and in the Qumran archive (CD XIV 20; 1QS VI 2; 4Q 26:1 3, 3). See M. Black, *An Aramaic Approach to the Gospels and Acts*, 2nd ed. (Oxford: Clarendon, 1954), 102; and M. Wilcox, "Mammon," in *ABD*, ed. David Noel Freedman (New York: Doubleday, 1992), 4:490.

4 Literally "eternal tents." We have a plural for singular in Psalm 84:2: *mah yĕdîdôt miškenôtekā* (plural) = "how lovely is your dwelling" (singular).

5 Rudolph Bultmann, *The History of the Synoptic Tradition*, trans. J. Marsh (Oxford: Clarendon, 1968), 196–97. Also see Joachim Jeremias, *The Parables of Jesus*, rev. ed. (London: SCM, 1963), 186; and Fitzmyer, *Gospel according to Luke X–XXIV*, 1126.

6 H. J. Cadbury, "A Proper Name for Dives," *JBL* 81 (1962): 399–401.

7 Speculation about the rich man's name is generally traced back to Hugo Gressmann's proposed parallels in his *Vom reichen Mann und armen Lazarus: Eine literargeschichtliche Studie* (Berlin: Königliche Akademie der Wissenschaften, 1918). More recently, see Fitzmyer,

Gospel according to Luke X–XXIV, 1130–31; R. E. Hock, "Lazarus and Mycellus: Greco-Roman Backgrounds to Luke 16:19–31," *JBL* 106 (1987): 447–63; R. E. Hock, "Lazarus and Dives," in *ABD* 4:266–67; J. R. Donahue, *The Gospel in Parable* (Philadelphia: Fortress, 1988), 167–70; and R. Bauckham, "The Rich Man and Lazarus: The Parable and the Parallels," *NTS* 37 (1991): 227–28. The rabbinic story about Ma'yan the rich tax collector and the poor scholar can be found in the Jerusalem Talmud (*Sanh.* 6:23c and Hag. 2:77d).

8 On the ossuaries, coffin-like containers in which the bones of the deceased were preserved in a kind of second burial, see Fitzmyer, *Gospel according to Luke*, 1131; C. A. Evans, *Jesus and the Ossuaries* (Waco, TX: Baylor University Press, 2003).

9 For more on Hades, see Simon Hornblower and Antony Spawforth, eds., *The Oxford Classical Dictionary*, 3rd ed. (Oxford: Oxford University Press, 1996), 661–62. The parable provides no basis for the assumption that Hades is here an intermediate rather than final state, as Joachim Jeremias states in *The Parables of Jesus*, 184–85.

10 Examples of this belief in the special significance of the number five can easily be verified. Examples from Luke's Gospel include the following: at the feeding of the five thousand, the people are arranged in groups of fifty and nourished with five fishes (Luke 9:13–14); in the parable of the grateful debtors, one owed five hundred and the other fifty denarii.

11 See R. F. Collins, "Lazarus," in *ABD* 4:265–66; and K. Pearce, "The Lucan Origins of the Raising of Lazarus," *ExpT* 96 (1985): 359–61. Many years ago, R. Dunkerley stated it categorically: "I find it quite impossible to accept this idea of coincidence. Here are two stories, in each of which a man named Lazarus dies. In one case a request is made that he may return after death to convince his contemporaries and to bring them to repentance, but permission is refused. In the other case the man *is* raised and *does* return and some of the people believe him and some do not." "Lazarus," *NTS* 5 (1958–59): 321–27.

12 F. V. Filson, "Who Was the Beloved Disciple?," *JBL* 63 (1949): 83–88; F. V. Filson, "Beloved Disciple," in *ABD*, ed. David Noel Freedman (New York: Doubleday, 1992), 1:378–79.

13 The rich man only asks for the return of Lazarus to visit his five brothers like a ghost (Luke 16:30), but in denying the request, Abraham speaks of his resurrection from the dead (16:31; *ean tis ek nekrōn anastē*).